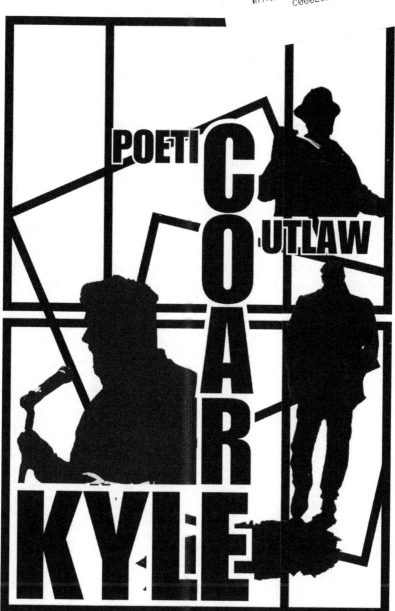

Poetic Outlaw

Kyle Coare

Other works by Kyle Coare.

Poetry

Prisoner of the mind
Prisoner of the heart
The night watchman*
Seasons*
Lone wolf*
Headfirst into the storm*
In shadows*
Torn pages: Scraps of midnight*
Endless nightmares*
Carpe noctem*

Short Stories

Midnight tales 1: Arty's tale

Non-Fiction

A brief history of video games*

All available from Amazon
in both Paperback and Kindle editions
*Also available in Hardback

FOUR 239

Acknowledgements

I want to thank everyone that has given me their love and support.
My family, always first and foremost.
I wouldn't be the man I am without your guidance, love, and honesty.
Accepting my flaws, listening to me ramble on. Trying to make sense of the million and one thoughts that are jostling for space.
Steve, you will be missed. You always inspired me, kept me firing and I'm sure you, dad, and all the other numerous people we've lost will be enjoying the music of the universe.
To the Some-Antics crew, simply put, I wouldn't have been doing this without you. Sammy who I am bankrupting one book at a time!
Jazmine who has inspired a lot of fun poems, and really interesting discussions and offered invaluable help and constructive criticism whilst putting together this collection.
As has Ellie, the thoroughly well-deserved champion of Some-Antics slam 2023. A genuine good heart with some of the most amazing poetry I've had the joy of reading and hearing. You always make me smile and given me valuable feedback and so much help and your poetry inspires me to want to be better.
Literally everyone at Get Mouthy, Carolina who always creates such a great atmosphere, and all the amazing poets and audiences.
You all inspire me and it is a true delight seeing you all grow as poets and performers. The whole point of Get Mouthy was to create a space where we could connect as humans, share our feelings and emotions and to grow like flowers, and to say if you have never got up on a stage then we will help, because we want to hear all stories and voices.
Sharena Lee Saati, a great poet that I read daily, who puts on events over the internet and in Bradford, who just inspires me from a far.
There are countless other names. For a reclusive, agoraphobic socially anxious poet I'd have never believed any of this only a handful of years ago.
All of you that have read my work, watched my videos, taken the time to comment or share something I've created, without you my work is just words, you give them the magic.
Thank you everybody, and please try to support your local poets, buy their books, go to open mic nights and soak up the atmosphere.
The world would be poorer without them.

Peace, Love & Poetry.
Kyle

ONE

**Poetry is love in words
a soft blown silent kiss
which makes the world slowly turn**

A poet's word

Words flow out
in scratched handwriting.
Evaporating like sunburnt tears.
They just drift,
swiftly lifting
through the air.
Blowing in the breeze.
They never find
empty inviting ears.
Only me
down on my knees.

A poet's words
are more than
letters tied together,
they are emotions
we share forever.
The fruits
we pluck free
from the
tree of memory.

Under the midday sun
they shimmer
like a swimmer
pushing through
coursing waters.
They sink and rise,
a visual mirage
before your eyes.
Wavy heat haze furrowed air.
Lost words that we
can no longer hear.

A poet's words
are not just talk.
They are dreams,
through which we walk.
Seeing all the intricacies,
being able to appreciate
the delicacies.

Words flutter free
like birds.
Just here to visit
before moving on,
never landing
for long.
Leaving behind
mere snippets,
memories
of a song.

A poet's words
are important.
They can be
the spark
that ignites a fire
in the heart.
They can bring
a loved one
back to life
and make bad memories
fall apart.

Yelped howls to a silent moon

The wolf sits,
cowering,
shivering, scared.
Air stained with memories.
Fear
coated
in yesterday's furs.
Since he started to walk alone,
the pathways have twisted,
taken turns
in directions unknown
and now he feels
even more alone.
In this ever decreasing
forest of closing trees.
He can barely breathe.
Roots tangled around roots,
trying to get a grip
on torn padded paws.

Expectations rained,
then sank
into the mud
just as quick.
Fur matted
with blood.
Skin clinging
to his bones.
The wolf howls.
Sorrowful sounds,
but only the trees
and air so misty,
hear his whelped misery.

The moon,
his guide,
still glides
across his eyes at night,
but now the years
have made his vision
less bright.
The tears have blurred
his sight
into a bleary mess.

Should he have just followed the pack?

No. The wolf thinks.
A glimmer of life
in teary eyes still sits.
I have to walk my own path.
The crowd doesn't have my back
and I know the story needs me.
It needs me to find
where I'm supposed to be.

A lifetime within a dream

Stuck in a dream
for what seems
like a lifetime.
Out of sight.
Out of mind.
I swim through
the channels,
waterways to hideaways.

I follow
the programming.
Coastal stop overs
into long, lazy days.
I witness forever
and I see yesterday.
All in the same moment.
As it all
fades away.

I'm stuck
in a dream
or is this
a nightmare.

Repeat.

I'm stuck
in a dream
or is this
a nightmare.
The constant marching feet.
The sound
of the war drums beat.
The aching tear ducts
too full, they crumble to dust.

Can't escape.
I'm stuck
in this otherworldly state.
A twist of fate, the one
that walks this place
has gone astray.
My mind arrays
flicking
over images.
Fire dancing a mental affray.
I'm stuck in a
dream or nightmare
that won't go away.

Is this a dream
or is this a nightmare?
Repeat
I5 thi5 4 dr34m
or i5 th1s 4 n1ghtm4r3?

The images 0uts1d3.
ar3 starting t0 scare.
The visi0ns that appear.
on my TV scr33n
Are making m3 aw4re
of what is happening
3ls3wher3.
I'm glitch1ng.
My head twitching,
m3nt4l footprints sticking
and I can't stop the
thoughts from itching.

Curse of the lonesome poet

It's the curse of the lonely poet,
can't get out of the place to which he fled.
Stuck, lost inside his head.
The screams he can no longer shout,
barely resonate.
Bouncing back
from blank slate,
walls of hate,
like a black hole
of self-doubt.

The curse of the lonely poet.
Destined to live
in the space
between the ears.
A grey matter maze
of frustration, anger and tears.
Of love lost,
found,
then lost again,
a never-ending cycle of pain.

The curse of the lonely poet.
Spare his heart the agony
of a slow break.
It is too much
for this old man to take.
He writes his words to all.
Who will hear?
Would anyone call
if he was the one to fall?

The curse of the lonely poet,
to walk the long path through
forests and storms,
across mountains and chasms.
To sail the vast oceans,
to swim in rivers and lakes.
Dragged along on the fluid emotions.
His mind a liquid state.

The curse of the lonesome poet
to walk this lonely planet,
always seeking.
Barely speaking.
Always in search,
of that one special soul.
The one
that will make
him whole,
give his words meaning.
Start his rickety heart beating.

Honouring the four walls

Whiling away the hours,
turning the hands on the clock,
to make time move quicker,
but time keeps a steady pace,
as pulse races with
anticipation to see
where this wandering path
will lead today.

Twiddled thumbs
don't make the hour come
any quicker.
Frittered moments
flutter by but never
seem any swifter.
Whittled minutes
weaved into wistful wonderings
won't make time pass, it just kindles fires.
Enabling embers,
energetic imagery
to break free,
but time doesn't move
any more quickly.

Wasteful hours
honouring these four walls.
I sprawl out and put my faith
in the ceiling to share
with me some insight,
but inside thoughts
never release. Just keep you
under lock and key,
wearing away at your sanity.

I tore the clock
from its
nail marked spot,
that incessant
ticking noise
had to stop.
The rot had started
to climb the walls,
as would my thoughts,
if I had any thoughts at all.
Is this how downfall feels?
Or just another night
where time ticks to a crawl.

Coffee-stained notes

Coffee-stained notes.
Rings, like black holes
pulling the words in.
To soak, in bitter
caffeine-tinged seas.
Bygone days of memory.
Words, handwritten. Lilting
towards the elliptical chasm.
A vast canyon of darkness
for them to dive within.
To coat themselves
in the sticky coffee residue
and create a whole new scent
for the story to be perfumed through.

The words explore further ashore.
Across lined parchment floors,
until they reach a place
where the ground doesn't extend,
only the vastness of space expands.
Where the lines stop,
and the paper trail ends.
Letters peer precariously over
torn worn-out edges,
wondering will they
ever make the cover
or spend eternity
teetering on slippery ledges.
These letters and words
only want to be seen.
To be more than images
on a paper screen.

So, the weary words
wander worlds,
wherever will they go?
They wonder this themselves.
Pondering over future shelves,
but for now, where the story flows
even they don't know,
but the coffee ring remains,
creating a looped view.
Rivers of arabica bean brew,
rippled over the aged yellow page,
to create a stage
for the words to portray,
to perform, to play.
A story.
A sip of coffee
on a mist sullied morning
and its back to
work for the day.

Children of midnight's light

Sometimes you have to stop running
from the moonlight.
Stop fearing the twilight,
let those nightmares wash over you,
waves of midnight.
Waves of grim vagaries that may cause fright.
In those early hours,
where daylight is hidden from sight.
Silken liquid terror starts to ooze.
Seeping through every groove,
like moonbeams
on a reflective river surface.
Into every pore, across your skin.
Stop running from bad dreams,
Nothing in here is as bad as it seems.

Sometimes we have to wrap ourselves in midnight.
Let the darkness cling tight.
A blanket against the outside,
a blanket against the things
that should cause flight.
Wrap ourselves in this shawl,
a barrier against nightfall.
Create a bubble
from the true terrors inside.
The ones that are not concerned with monsters
nor crooked reanimated old bones,
but with the fear that sits with us in our minds.
In our homes.
The fear of outside lives.
The fear of feeling the glow of red cheeks,
the fear of feeling like some kind of freak,
for having a view of the world
that is your own observation.
Beautiful and unique.

We are the children of midnight's light.
The ones who sit in darkness
to feel alive.
We walk this phantom land
between twilight
and dawns eerie early glow.
We live like creatures scurrying
through the land below.
Eyes attuned to the full moon
and the sheet of night that blows,
consuming the light before it flows.
We are the order of the stars,
the orchestrations of dust from afar.
We are the children,
the everlasting stories
that will sing
our forever song.

Fog of melancholia

When melancholia rolls in
like a teasing fog,
across my thoughts.
When clouds are painted
in a spectrum of grey,
and the tainted blue sky is
threatening to tear my day
in two. I let my thoughts blow away.
When low is the only way
my mood will go,
I take myself to the city,
where the lights always glow.

When polythene fear
clings tightly to my skin,
and my weary thoughts
are wearing thin,
I take to the place
where the electric flow
of fluorescent light sinks in.
I like to watch people
going to and fro, dancing
under the moons ancient glow.

I wear a novocaine smile
like my brain has been pulled,
my mind lulls my thoughts into sleep.
Empty and dull.
I listen to the call,
the city, she sings to me.
To walk her concrete caverns,
to feel the pulse race
through asphalt veins beneath my feet.
To sense the essence of life that never stalls.

When my mind is stood on the brink
of the dark abyss of emptiness.
My thinking is a mess.
My opinions sinking into deep mud,
and I'm feeling stuck.
I let the shine of streetlights guide.
I let the solid ground be the foundation
to my climb, I put one foot
in front of the other,
and let the city welcome me
like a loving mother.

Holding a grimace at bay

Crying at night
so that his hurt was
hidden, downtrodden.
Out of sight.
No-one could listen
to the whistling
pain inside,
that echoed
through this shattering
crystalline heart.

I stand outside, looking in.

The clockface shimmers before ripping apart.
I'm staring through distorted mirrors.
I see pain manifesting over
every bone, into every moan.
Everything I'd ever known.
Gone. Alone in an empty home.

Another mirror, another time.
I see him smile,
but it's holding a grimace at bay,
barring it entry to his face.
Turn the lock, throw away the key.
Drown with me. He thinks.
Sinking into this deep amber sea.
We float with the ice.
We float down the drain,
like pissing in the rain,
it's all worthless
in this sea of pain.

Through another reflective surface
I see dead eyes.
I see rivers of blood rise.
I see yellow skin. Sunken tears
drowning within this dead sea.
Red tides erupting.
I want to smash the mirrors.
Scream. To sort it out quickly.
I want to bang on the glass,
say stop. Fast.
But it's too late.
Too much time had passed.

I see the man regain his feet,
weak, broken, dazed.
Amazed at the new sight,
long days ahead. *Speak.*
I try but the glass muffles
the words when I cry.
But I see a glimpse of recognition
as he stares deeper into the reflection,
and realises he can recover from this.
At least he can if I exist.

I see sadness in your eyes

I see hurt caught
in the lies of your smile.
Lines that point up,
but are feeling dragged down.
I've felt the weariness
from too many miles.
When the world feels corrupt,
and you feel you're starting to drown.
I've worn your frown,
to get a sense of the intense pain,
so that I can understand
what you are feeling,
and I've worn my own frown
from my own pain.
Knowing that through it all
we can rise up again.

I see sadness in your eyes.
It betrays the mask
you wear trying to hide
the tears that you've cried,
but they shine
like neon lines
cracking your cheeks.
I've felt the hurt release
It's vicelike grip.
When you've had
a chance to speak
and instead
just let your words slip.

And when those words
reach the air
electricity rips,
a storm raises neck hairs.
Intense energy flips.
Now the power is within.
The words you spray
make the world spin
the right way,
for just a few moments
of this dreary day.

I don't claim
to know your pain.
Everyone's rain
hits a unique way,
but I offer a hand
is what I say.
My smile sometimes
fades too, and in truth
I sometimes feel
I'm drowning under the swell,
but I'll hold the umbrella for you
until I walk the fires of hell.

Over light beam playgrounds

The deep thick blue
of the twilight sky,
rippled with duvet clouds
to curl up inside,
whilst pillows swirl
over the light beam
playgrounds,
the loving moon
so carefully provides.

The sweet embrace
of that night-time wonder.
The heavens above
on which we ponder.
The place where dreams
will circle and fly.
The palatial bed
where you can rest down your head
and let your eyes close tight.
Hoping to catch
some mystical flight
to otherworldly lands.
Dusty sands with sparkling delight.

The darkening tones,
not fearful, nor distressing.
Just resting.
Not paining or contesting,
but soothing and caressing.
Slowly undressing your mind.
The way the moon
highlights the trees,
the beautiful canopy.
A wisp of white,
freckled with green leaves.

The listless way
the light slowly plays,
dancing, it sways
down darkened alleyways.
Across fields, and houses,
up towers and mountains.
Glistening
in the flourishing display
of glittery water,
as the old fountain
sporadically sprays.

Love roams the lush undergrowth

A tree of thoughts
grows outwardly,
reaching towards you,
and from
your mind
branches entwine
with mine.

I long to feel
our words speak,
a dream.
Becoming tangled
in your vines.
In the deep pine groves
where love roams
through the
lush undergrowth.
To feel our words
light as a feather,
as if tethered
by some unspoken force
pulling them together.

Where softly, they huddle close,
somewhere in this
boundless expanse,
before swirling
in an airy dance.
Yours taking
the high notes,
mine
the deeper undertones.

I long, as I have
for so long,
to be held
by your words.
To be carried along,
like they are a pathway
guiding me on.
Showing me the way,
to the greatest honour
a man can hope upon.

I wish to be
a kiss on the breeze,
your everlasting memory.
To be someone that
makes you
as weak at the knees
as you make me,
like I'm a ship
on undulating seas.
Feeling the waves
making me unsteady,
as I wish to
lay at your feet.

The edges of my voice

It sometimes feels
like words across space
are intrinsically linked.
Things inked
in my scrawled handwriting
crawl towards the words
you so delicately print.
And words that you speak
seek out the edges of my voice,
crawling in, to find some peace.
Two souls on a sea alone,
vast distances between
and a hazy mist,
hiding us from view.
Making us the unseen.
Sailing in a long-forgotten dream
that we have yet to see.

It's so easy to get lost
in this darkening soup.
The light.
Unable to break through,
but then your soulful words
are ladled in.
Cutting through the bitter stew.
Spoon-feeding light into the view.
Making joy
a truth,
instead of just a story
we spoke of
as little girls and boys.

It sometimes feels
like your words are sent
to pierce a hole directly through
my heart and into my soul,
and in reverse my words
are cursed to forever
speak to this silent universe.
Whispering words
for unlistening ears.
All so I don't let on, that inside
I'm shivering in fear.
For if I ever let you near.
I'd never be able to let you go again.

Moon-shaped bookmark

I keep a moon-shaped bookmark
to part the pages of my life. To mark
the sections I want to revisit,
tales of happiness and love,
moments when secret smiles shined
from the sky above, moonlight fingers
stroking my hair, the wind swept
pages breathing life into my lungs.

I use my moon-shaped bookmark,
to see where I am at the end of a day,
to light new paths I may wish to embark,
to part seas that may block the way.
My moon-shaped guide
to a life I chose to live.

My moon-shaped bookmark
keeps the good and bad days apart.
It divides my days into light and dark,
into heart and hurt. It starts my night
with a kiss of love, it ends with light
streaming down from the sun.

When sleep is distant
and relaxing is a struggle,
when my mind won't quieten
from the noise
of thoughts that rustle,
I read until my eyes start to droop.
The bookmark of the moon
lighting the pages, before it sees my eyes
and dims to say, *'go to sleep call it a day.'*

Fragments of yesterday

Fragments of dreams,
that's what the day has been.
Fragments of heartaches.
Pieces torn free,
pieces that once made me,
now just float away in the breeze.
Fragments of yesterday,
splinter through the wind,
stick into my mind,
too deep to cut them free.
Fragments of dreams,
that's all I could be.
Memories of melodies
caught in the breeze.
Fragments of yesterday.
Tales told in sand.
Fragments of stories,
I once held in my hand.

To those long-forgotten dreams

To those
long-forgotten dreams.
I let you go. Left to fade
under the strawberry rain,
to become fiction.
Whilst I lay
letting the sweetness
take any bitter taste away.

To those wavy daydreams
that seeped into the air,
you became the raindrops on my page.
Teardrops of my heart.
Every moment fills a piece of my journal.
A testimonial of where my
journey started and where it fell.

To those fleeting figments of fantasy
that once enticed me,
that kept me tied
to their golden sunsets.
You became the ink that stained
the corners of the paper castles,
like the tears that dripped
from the corners of my eyes.
You set forth dragons
with fires that rage,
you lit within me a passion
to burn my heart onto the page.

Regret doesn't sit so well
on this old tongue.
For the story to turn right
sometimes takes
things to seemingly go wrong.
Obstacles make
the chapters sizzle.
We need adversary
to create the necessary fizzle.
To rise you must first fall.
My past made me.
Every stumble has been
a wake-up call.
Forget looking
back in hurt
at all those lost smiles.
Look back instead
at the moments
that made it all worthwhile.

Misted windows into the dream world

I wake up in a cold sweat,
knees held, strapped to my chest.
Hugged as tightly as a lover,
but I must confess
my body doesn't bend like this.
I'm panting for breath.
What had scared me so?
I gaze into the misted windows
of the dream world, still visible
but fading quickly.
I peered within,
only seeing a fleeting shadow
bleed into the darkness slickly.

Terrified,
I try to prise my fingers apart,
set tight
like a vice or clamp.
To free my legs
from my grip,
If I stay in this
position much longer,
I'll end up bent double
with ice in my veins
and a terrible bout of cramp,
but those fingers are locked,
like if I were to let my body spread,
then the only outcome would be
to wind up dead.

I sense I'm not alone.
When loneliness
is your closest companion,
you can feel when someone
else is in the room,
like the air is charged.
Any movement will send
a spark to your heart,
stopping you dead.
Leaving you staring
at the deadlights ahead.

I glance at the clock.
Expecting hours
to have circled past,
but it was less than five minutes
since I'd opened
my eyes last.

"This is going to be
a bloody long night."

I say to nobody.

"Yes, it is"

They reply.

Fear evolves

Fear changes.
It evolves
as time edges
ever onwards, and the world revolves.

As a child I believed
I'd be eaten alive by the earth,
drowning in quicksand
as it creeps, scratching at my eyes.
Spontaneous human combustion
would burn me to a crisp,
as a flickering flame licks,
hot and fiery at my fearful face.
I wonder would it taste the tears?
and would they make it
grimace in pain?

As a child
I feared acid rain.
I screamed in high pitched tones
at the thought of my skin slipping
from my bones, pain ripping,
dripping into a liquid sludge,
but then I remembered
that in my fears, the piranhas
had already taken my skin,
even my ears.
So, my bones were
the least of my worries.

As a child I feared
the monster beneath my bed,
which was odd as my bed didn't have legs.
He would grab at me as I slept,
with fingers sharp and serrated.
Oh, the tears I wept,
but that fear soon abated.
As to sit under my bed
any monster would have to be
as thin as a sheet.

I feared the Bermuda triangle.
A place I didn't expect to survive,
yet so far, I've managed just fine.
Just avoided travelling
across those three lines.
I feared monsters
that lurked.
The hushed silence
as we walked past
that creepy church.

But I never feared the darkness,
and now I fear people
more than any of this.
I fear losing my voice,
feeling alone.
I fear
leaving my home,
and not being
able to cope.

Licence to write

A licence to write,
killer lines,
execute on sight.
A licence to make
audiences gasp
in delight,
or squirm
in their seats.
Tears flooding
their eyes.
A licence
to excite,
or put wrongs
right.
A licence
to use your pen
to fix a world
that often feels
a little broken.

A licence
to let words flow,
feeling them erupt out
like rivers of lava
from an angry volcano.
We pick apart our lines,
to feel the way
they sit in the mind,
to try to make them
stick tightly,
a sticking plaster, slightly askew,
to fit every mood nicely,
or at least some superglue to fix any
thoughts that have become broken
or just slightly unscrewed.

It isn't something
we take lightly.
This heavy pen
so mighty.
It's something
we caress.
Harness close
to our chests.
Embrace
in times of loneliness.
Feed it, nurture it,
invest our love.
We give our pen
so much.
We open wounds
to fill it with blood.
We cry on its nub,
to sate its thirst.
We cling on tight,
when the world
feels it is about to burst.
Then we scribble down
the resulting verse.

Shrink-wrapped fear

Overthink.
Overthink.
Into bed I sink,
as thoughts start to scream.
Infesting my dreams,
creating nightmare seas
from mere rivers or streams.
Overthink.
Overthink.
When thoughts start to link.
It's hard to clear out the bilge water,
harder still to plug the holes.
You can't keep on rowing
with cracks in the portholes,
and a hull filling with water, black as ink.
The boat starts to sink.

Overthink.
Overthink.
The waters are deep,
and more thoughts start flowing.
It's starting to leak into my skull.
How can I keep on going
when my mind is too full?
Overthink.
Overthink.
Bail the water.
Plug the leak.
Warped wood
starting to creak.
Overthink.
Overthink.
About anything
except this shrink-wrapped fear
that obscures everything.

Overthink.
Overthink.
Now my sense
has taken a running jump
from the brink.
Taken a dive into
the deep dark drink.
Overthink.
Overthink.
Words pull me down.
Overblown mind
starting to drown
under foamy waves.
I wait to be saved.
Then kick my legs free.
Surface teasing me.
Tantalisingly out of reach.
What I wouldn't give
for a sandy beach
and some company.

Tiptoe

You tiptoed
across my heart strings.
Bare foot.
Soft skin.
Balancing
on tender
frayed
threading.
The vibrations ripple,
tickling awake
my once dormant heart.
I feel the treat of dancing stars
twinkling to share this new start.

The shrill sound of songbirds,
singing songs to the sky.
Songs of a flower that is budding,
and will blossom in time.
Your fingers entwine with mine
and we wrap our roots together.
Twisted hungry vines, pulses flow between
like a dawn chorus along a telephone line.

I feel that surge flow through us,
like electric currents
through fairy lights of love.
Making us glare, brighter
than the moon sat shyly miles above.
That look in those searching eyes,
staring deep inside, trying to pry apart
the very atoms of my mind.
So, I open my blinds, let you wander in.

This world of mine
is not used to much company,
but it is cosy
and the seating is comfy.
So, pull up a chair,
and what's mine
I'll share.

Our minds connect,
like two pieces of a small jigsaw,
as I feel you dancing
twinkle toed across my synapses.
I am given a brief look
into the worlds that flow
through your minds lengthy corridors,
and I want what I saw. I want to explore
the world in your head.
A world painted
in so much colour, so vivid.
When mine is just shades
of blues and reds.
So, take me where you go
show me what you see,
I won't ever let go,
if you'll promise
to keep a hold of me.

Where seas flow and the river rages

I see so much beauty
in the lines of your mind.
The outside beauty
often gets outshined
by the majestic glow
you hold inside.
How can someone
hold so much light
and not know?
How can somebody hold
So much light
and not ignite,
burning away
into the midnight sky.
If you reached out,
embers to the touch.
I'd fizzle into dust.
My body would die
but my heart and soul would fly.

My vision blurs
when my eyes glance.
It's like a picture of perfection.
Too much for my eyes to see,
so, they shade the view.
Only allowing me to see the truth
through the words you use.
I would become a million shadows
if your light cast itself upon me.
All the darkness would seep away
like rain down a gurgling drain,
into the crazy paving streets,
into the cracks and soil beneath.

But the outside
is merely a preview,
a book cover,
with so many stories
held within.
I want to tease
the pages with fingers
eagerly caressing
the edges.
Letting the words
flow across my palms,
staining my fingers
with loves blessings.
Feeling every glowing moment,
as my mind witnesses
all of the charms
held within those pages.
All I want is to be held
in those arms
as I fade into the ages.

They say beauty is only skin deep,
but this is not true, there is beauty
in the very core of you.
Something uniquely tattooed to your soul.
It's deeper than any man-made hole,
brighter than any glimmer of gold.
More priceless than diamonds or gems.
It can't be seen through any fancy lens.
Just on the edges of your pen.
On the words you let float onto pages,
something drawn through ages,
where the seas flow
and the river rages.

Pull the trigger on a blown kiss

I wear my heart
on the sleeve
of a book,
covered in love.
Hearts drawn,
take 12 paces
and turn.

Pull the trigger on a blown kiss,

I'll fall.
I'll give my all to you.
Every part of me.
My infatuation
scrawled in notes,
my desire in writing,
written in fire
to light up the heavens.

I would burn brighter than stars
to let you know.
I'd relight your sun
if it ever entered
a deep-freeze.
I'd carve mountainous
hearts in snow,
I'd twist rivers
to bend into words
that flow.

As long as you never break my heart.

I put forth my words
in poetic verse,
painted all over
museums of love,
cathedrals of hope,
temples of togetherness.

I wish upon shooting stars.
Throw coins in magical fountains.
If I could,
I'd move mountains,
making the wind
sing through them.
I'd plant trees to move
the whistling frequency,
until it sings in human voice.

I'd make the waves on the sea
match the rhythm of my heart.
To play a beat,
and I'd line up shells
until you hear that sea,
singing its loving tune from me.

To see you smile,
to feel that look in your eye.
To feel you close by,
holding me
when my own tears cry.
I'd give anything.
As long as you don't
break my heart
and let it die.

How are you?

How are you...

I'm fine I reply.
It's easier than trying
to explain why
the grey sky
is making you
feel like crying inside.

I'm fine, I'm okay.

It's never I'm lonely,
or I'm feeling a bit low today.

Can't seem
to let those words swim.
So, we drown them,
let them sink deeper in.

It's like there is a mental block,
around a pad-locked door
marked with a sign,

*"don't enter, here is where
depressed thoughts are stored."*

It's always the same line,
the same refrain.
Everything is tickety boo.
I'm not under a dark cloud
and it isn't starting to rain.

You let the sounds
inside cry instead,
and you can't clear
the thoughts in your head,
but I'm okay, I'm fine
you relay over and over,
because you know
that these depressive
thoughts will go
and trying to find
the right words,
is like trying
to find a speck of sugar
on a ground full of snow.

Some days just hearing a voice
raises the mood, if only a little.
It makes the day bearable.
Just hearing someone else speak,
hearing their stories, fresh and unique,
makes you feel less bleak.
Fills the reserves with just enough juice
to know that you will get through,
and that there is someone out there
that cares about you.

The glamour and the glitz

The glamour and the glitz.
Neon lights hit,
but beneath sits
a layer of grime.
Dirt is never hard to find.
Cold and dark.
Smiling faces
a thing only remembered from home,
but here you only ever feel alone.
The leers and stares,
as you take the apples and pears,
leaves a stain that no washing will cleanse away.

Don't forget home
whilst you walk
these angry streets alone.
Amid the dusty streetlights
and the neon highs.
Don't be fooled into believing
that the shit is golden
or that this city is breathing.
It's an undead nightmare
that keeps on bleeding, no heart is truly beating.

When you stare at pillars and towers,
big, high skyscrapers piercing the sky.
A shard of glass and iron ripping a hole up there.
Don't be fooled,
or try to hide your despair.
This is a lair
of cheats and devils,
whose only cares
are about themselves
and their own personal wealth.

Jack used to rip,
every room is a pit
where someone has died,
had throats slit,
metaphorically
or literally,
they have seen their lives slip,
fading into
the bowels of hell.
Where transportation spits
dirt that gets ground in,
don't be fooled into thinking
that this is where soul is found.

Drink the poison to get merry,
take the pills
it will look more pretty
and forget about money,
you won't be left a penny.
In this hellish overblown city.
Overgrown with steel,
blocking sunbeams.
Where faces look
like Edvard Munch's scream
and the rest just stare
out into the distance
in a trance or a dream.

A rumble before a roar

We gentle types
have a river
surging inside.
Rolling,
crashing currents
urging our thoughts on.
Turbulent skies,
filled with clouds,
all clashing for space.
Building up charge,
to unleash a blinding rage.
The brightest fiercest
blast of lightning,
direct to the page.

We may seem
slow, cautious,
uninterested, lost,
but inside. My gosh.
It's a whole wall of sounds.
Vying to get out.
Trying to make themselves heard
over the other sounds,
rushing and pushing about.
When someone hands us a mic and says
speak your mind, say your truth,
give us your view,
let us feel the world within you.
We let the waves push aside,
and let our message start to shout.
Little ripples become waves
as the pulse rushes out.

To some we appear brittle,
fragile, frail and weak.
Sometimes we find it
hard to speak.
We work better with
a book in hand,
our minds connect
with the words within.
Then urge the words to
flow into you.
But don't let appearances
cloud your mind. Obscuring the view.
I've walked through hell,
and from those fires
I arose,
with a strength
burning from my eyes
and the power of a thousand suns
sitting behind.

A rumble before a roar,
a slow trickle before a downpour.
I see you.
With your words so raw.
A war going on.
I know this song. I've heard it sung.
It's one I've sung to myself
when things are wrong.
We *are* the song that is sung.
We relight the fire in the sun.
I've seen your skies, from deep inside.
heard them call. Happily, I'd dive.
Into your rivers I'd fall.
To be by your side.
With our minds forever taken
on a magic boat ride.

A lone flower under moonless sky

In lines
of verse,
implanted hearts
soar.
Hidden messages
sent across
the universe
to explore.
Through the stars they roar.
To lay at your door.
A single flower grows
in the ground to show
that words mean more
than empty land
left hollow.

The flower
wasn't there
the day before.
It was seeded
from the sky that tore.
Emptied her tears
out over the ground,
soaked her soul
onto the floor.

The colours vibrant,
spoke of love
and guidance,
hope and truth,
lost moments
dreaming of you.

In words it lived,
where footprints stood.
Dug into
the soil and mud.
Breathed amid
the spaces left,
in the breaths between
our thoughts, bereft.

In every pause.
In the ripples waiting
whilst you
collect your thoughts.
The messages seep
into your dreams,
in those fleeting images seen.
You see the words
lit up bright,
like stars
upon a moonless night.

A glass dropped from on high

Called lazy
like you choose
to be so tired.
Drained of life,
with a fog over your mind.
Made to feel guilty.
Blamed.
Ashamed on the days
when you can't rise
from your bed,
like you have a zombie shaped weight,
hanging from a single hair, over your head.

And when that darkness
devours the light,
like a great mouth
chewing, making a meal
of your time.
It's so easy to lay in the dark. No spark.
Muscles tight,
bones feeling brittle and weak,
like a single knock
could shatter you.
A glass dropped from high.

You feel like a waste,
because the simple life
is so hard to follow.
Your mind feels hollow.
Just making it through a day
and ending up more
than just a shadow of you,
takes all the energy of the sun,
the stars and the moon too.

But you get called lazy
workshy, a waste of resources.
No discourse, you are just placed
on the rubbish pile,
because you don't conform
to the ordinary lifestyle.
Called idle, apathetic,
careless, inattentive.
Don't provide money for the rich,
so, what are you here for?
They say as you are
pushed out of the door.

Gatekeeper

Can we stop
with the gatekeeping?
Art, like beauty,
is in the eye of the beholder.
So, stop insisting
that your smeared lens
is the only way to see.
Beauty in art may sing
like a choir,
or it may hum
a slow drone,
slightly out of tune,
but with something
magical in the tones.

I've heard so many say,
but it's not poetry
or I don't like the artistry
this painter displays.
I'm not keen on this singers
song of choice.
It doesn't fit my tiny box.
It doesn't tick the box that
I've convinced myself this
art must consist of.
Art can be as delicate
as a sapling making its first
forays into the sun,
or as big and bold
as a mountainous tree
that's been around
since long before we were born.

It's okay to dislike the work,
but do you have to be a jerk?
Putting down the hours, the days, the weeks and years.
The searching through misty tears,
just trying to find the right way
to portray what it is that you are trying to convey.
Art can be like an ocean wave,
and crash onto the scene
like that wave upon a beach,
or it can be more meaningfully,
meandering like a stream,
slowly finding its ways into the cracks we leave.

Criticism is fair game,
ripping a person's heart out
to make you seem
like the only person
who understands art,
is not.
It's just bullying with a different name.
Advice is fair. To rip and tear is not the same.
Art doesn't have to be constrained by the past.
What came before is a guide,
but the way forward is a vast open frame.

Kindness isn't weak.
All you have to do is
think before you speak.
Would you like someone
to say these things to you?
Would it make you want to continue?
Without art we would be so much poorer.
It's the currency of love, of hurt and pain.
Within it we hold the truth our souls contain.

Better kept to the page

Those stuttered words
hang on my lips. Nearly slip.
Feeling friction.
as stumbling, they grip a tight hold.
Too scared to be heard,
they climb back inside.
Just fiction of the mind.
Timid, like a fox looking for
food in an autumnal downpour.

Those words still linger,
a thought once opened
can't be put away so easily,
and those stuttered words
would always be better kept
to a page. Never to be let out
of their paper cage.
I know my place, in this world
and to have that happy embrace
is a fantasy that can't exist.

My ears sigh.
Thankful that they
don't have to hear a reply.
My eyes just leak,
gazing off into the distance.
But my mind...
My mind is always
up to his own tricks.
Trying to make me fall
for his games.

So, I push my mind
into a faraway galaxy.
Why jeopardise good things
for misplaced chemistry?
Better to keep
that mind entertained,
in a place
of my own insanity,
but he is always there,
where shadows fall.
One step ahead of the game.
He knows what
I'm thinking after all.

Stuttered words
sometimes do slip.
Those muttered refrains take air.
Magic words
fall like a spectrum of rain,
a prism of shifting visions.

But then sometimes words fall,
because special is special,
and the future
is out of your control.

Beautiful eyes

You have
the most beautiful eyes.
The way you can see inside,
tears my heart in two.
I just want to kiss you.
Let your hair flow
freely through my fingertips,
I want to feel windswept hearts leaping.
I want to kiss your forehead,
whilst you are sleeping,
slipping into soft dreams.
I want to walk through
those dreams with you.

With you I feel at ease,
like my mind isn't away
flying over stormy seas.
With you I feel
weak at the knees
and my heartbeat ceases to hit
when the beats are expected.
It has its own rhythm
pounding in my head.
Making me long
to hold you tightly
in my arms instead.

You have
the most beautiful eyes.
Through them I can see inside.
See the person that makes me smile,
that lifts my mood stops my sighs.

You have the most beautiful eyes,
but they don't see me,
they think I'm somebody
that just passes your way.
They don't see
the way my heart sways,
staggering like I'm drunk
on your intoxicating rays.
When I am with you,
I want to dance
the darkness away.
Those beautiful eyes
don't see how
I want that magical feeling
to live inside every day.

You have
the most beautiful eyes.
I hope someday,
someone will see you
and those words will say
what you've always
wanted to hear.
I hope that they see
the beauty inside,
that makes you
so perfect.
I hope they give
you the life
that I could never
hope to find.
Because you are
so special,
loving
and kind.

Wreck in a trilby hat

I am a wreck
in a trilby hat,
wearing
yesterday's
faded dreams.
Carrying
a sack full
of regrets.
Basically,
I'm not all that,
but what I've got
is yours,
like a really
poor version
of Santa Claus.

I wear a book
to my chest,
instead of an S.
I'm not super.
I barely get out
without an uber,
but all I've got
I'll give it to you,
because I want
to see the world happy,
and when you smile
it's the whole world I see
shining through.

I don't want things.
Stuff doesn't excite me.
Money not on my list,
material doesn't give
that sense of bliss
which comes from love.
Not gifts or rewards,
but a warming kiss,
blown across
a frozen wilderness,
aimed at my lips,
would win almost
all the awards.

I'm a relic. Buried,
but I'm no treasure.
I'm just a bronze penny,
dug under the soil.
I'm nothing special,
but I am unique.
A one of a kind.
If you wipe away
the surface grime,
that bronze penny
might even shine.

A winter of frozen dreams

I'm watching
my happiness float away,
as a rain of melancholia
colours my vision grey.
I'm watching
as hope springs run dry,
like tears from lonely eyes.
I'm feeling the coldness
of a winter of empty dreams.
I shout to the sky.

Can I have some light,
a smile, some warmth?
Would it be wrong to ask
the flowers to bloom for me?
Would it be selfish
to wish for a less stormy sea?
If only for a few days, a week
just to feel some peace.

I'm tasting nothing but
that empty acrid nothingness in my gut.
Only replaced by the acid burns
as my stomach churns.
I'm pacing my mind,
as my legs have no motivation to walk.
I'm writing out lines
as my mouth has lost its ability to talk.
I'm feeling lost in a void.
People tend to avoid
those that are feeling deeply devoid.
So, I sit here getting
more and more paranoid.
Have I upset or annoyed?

Is it too big an ask
to not have to feel constantly
under my own personal attack?
From my own feelings
turning themselves on me
when I'm feeling flat.
Is it too much to ask
to want a day where
these questions don't
need to be asked?

A sea mist over a still beach

Anxiety twitches through veins,
frothing like acid
poured down a clogged drain.
Wrenching pain from deep within,
placing it on display,
in a glass case under lock and key,
for all the judgemental eyes to see.

It makes me feel.
Weak.
Frail.
Unstable on my own two feet.
Destined to fail.
It fills me with fear,
the kind that no nightmare
could dream of.
It overflows, spilling from my mind
like an overfilled cup.

Anxiety grips me close,
holding me like a comfort blanket
to ward off its own ghosts,
but anxiety walks away
when I set foot on the stage.
When I let my words
jump from the page,
to play their little games
with the air.

I couldn't see
the wonder in days,
when night had
always held so much sway.
My heart loves the night
and anxiety departs
when the sun goes away.
It leaves me, let's me swirl
through streets,
like sea mist over
a still beach.
As lights dance,
my shadow sashays
to the music that plays.

But then it soon returns.
Inside, my blood
bubbles and burns,
my mind's gears twist and turn.
I can't focus, my mind all at sea.
All I see are blurred, lost pictures of me.
Names and faces jostle for attention,
but it's no good,
I can't make connections.
Nothing makes sense,
I feel I'm entering a storm
all I can do is wait
for night to calm.

Ugly world

Violence on the rise,
splattered stuffed toys.
Caked in
rust coloured blood.
Innocence cries.
A tide
of uncertainty,
over unsteady seas.
This world can be
so very ugly.

I wish I could
paint some colour
into the scenery.
I'd blow
a strong breeze,
clearing the hazy hate away.
Leaving only
wide open seas,
instead of these
darkening shades
of grey tinged misery.

I'd wish upon
a shooting star,
throw all my coins
in a fountain.
Seek clovers of all kinds.
Searching low valleys
and high mountains, looking for hope
in this world of unease.
I'd row my boat
over unpredictable seas.
In hope to share,
to show that we care.

This world so ugly,
a hug is what it needs.
Warm away the coldness
that freezes hearts mid beat,
and echoes through
rhythms that no longer meet.
I wish for a world
where borders are never closed.
Where we don't let hate blind our eyes
and we can reopen the ones closed tight,
without raising our arms in fight.
So, they won't miss out
on all the wonders you can find,
and all of the people
with beauty living inside.

A bag blown on the wind

Paranoia painted
all over my face.
A dark dance
into the wilderness.
A last embrace,
with clear thought being
waved into the distance.
Some small talk,
in whispers,
which slither through
primed ears.
Walks on blisters.
Shivering.
Scared to tears.

Paranoia floats
like a bag blown
on heavy wind.
It swoops
into your face,
as you try to dodge
its smothering descent
into your personal space.
Not noticing
the looks of disgrace
peering inwards
from your own eyes
as you sigh
and frown to blustery skies,
hiding gaze from the crowds.

Paranoia leers,
peering into your mind to find
all of your personal fears.
Then displays them in a case,
for all to witness.
You shake
from the witless sense of injustice.
Feeling your fitness to be around
has vanished, self-punished
you plummet to the ground
like hailstones thrown
in angry outbursts from the clouds.

Paranoia breathes
foul scented breath.
Can smell its acrid scent,
like rotting meat and cigarettes
as I take
my next staggered step.
I feel it tingle
on the nape of my neck. It mingles
with the hairs bristling.
Fighting with my sanity
to find out who will be king,
and at the moment,
it is winning.

Leaden grey winter days

Slate grey rain
dampens my spirit,
blurring everything along with it.
A rainbow of misery.
A wash of gunmetal painted
over the cement-stained sky.
No colour passes this way.
All tainted in grey,
the hues and tones
all washed away.

A grim drain, gurgles
sucking the life
from the day, overflowing
with more frothing
puddles of ash-tinged sadness
to stain the streets,
as the hours fade
into the darkening leaden shade.
A nightfall smeared
with the charcoal remnants
of a sun left to wonder,
why it woke up at all.

Grey skies conspire,
whispering high above
the spires and telephone wires.
To circle. To taunt. The lands
they haunt
and stain with their
dreaded tin like rains.
Melancholy dyed
in stonewash floods,
leaving a place with no colour.
No good.

Galloping hooves

Thunder rumbles
like galloping hooves
across the fearful sky.
Bright light
ignites into a
blinding sight.
A lightning strike.
A lone tree.
Alone and lonely, stood
in open fields of memory.
The rain starts to flood.

The scraping sound,
crashing around
like furniture dragging across
the heavenly waiting rooms above,
and those rooms
have sprung a leak.

Down here
on this spherical ship
sailing through space.
The waters don't seem to cease.
We just hide in place,
waiting for the rains to abate.
Waiting for some peace.

But that lonely tree,
still stands alone.
Just a smoky ghost
of memory.

Deep waters were here to stay

I could feel the tension in the air,
rippling through my muscles.
Every joint flared,
every tendon, flayed and raw.
My head was amid a long civil war,
with rockets flaming through my hair
and the sound of automatic rifles
deafeningly near.
Hovering close, I saw through
dirt covered windows. A cloud,
as black as ink
and it was spreading,
like a spilled well
upon a blotter page.

As the dark clouds covered my sky
I closed my eyes.
And I listened.
As the screams of rain ripped through the air,
streams slipping down windowpane,
I heard hearty laughter of thunder
and a hammer of pain,
as blinding lightning strikes
burned through eyelids fused together tight.
As I lay, I fought demons in my head,
walked through hell with feet of lead
and awoke, sweat drenched in my bed.
Day born of night.

I needed to breathe
clean air
into soot filled lungs.
I could hear
mournful birdsong
being sung.
I opened the door,
and a boat floated there.
The deluge had been and gone,
but now deep waters were here to stay.
I would have to brace the cold and swim
if I wanted to get away,
or grow old and stay within
slowly withering
into a reminder of another day.

In blotchy newsprint ink

It hits you, if you read between
the lines. The fiction. The soundbite
insights into the minds
of our supposed leaders.
See their deeds, conspiratorial,
they lead. Never by example,
but almost always by greed.
See their lies clear as day
for all to read on the blood-stained pages,
Read what they say
and what they do not say.

If they were to look in the mirror,
under that star we call the sun,
their times would be undone
by the bad things they've done.
Independent thought would
start to take hold, our guardians no longer
in control. Mail would pile up daily.
The news of the world would be about
our leaders decay. Express trains would
spread the news quicker than a telegraph,
and we would stand tall in the aftermath.

But we fall for their lines.
The lies hidden in plain sight
in blotchy newsprint ink.
This corrupt system
is starting to stink.
It hits you,
like a baseball bat of truth
around the head.

Wham!!

The thoughts you
thought you had,
were just noise.
Implanted through
things you read.
They dull down our instinct
to ask questions,
they want us brain dead,
flaked out watching
Tik Tok instead.

And in the void that surrounds
they pump sounds.
You are not enough,
you don't amount to much,
you need to be more.

Consume, consume, consume.

Now let's have a little war. Follow the herd.
Don't question what you heard.
Your orders are clear the enemy is near.

Fear, fear, fear.

Consume.

The bomb drops

And boom!

Oily slick silence surrounds.
I'm alone,
drowning in this world of words
and no one is reading along.

TWO

**Time spent all alone can hurt
invest in a pen
words can heal wounds left open**

Anti-muse awakens

Stumbling. Twirling through the night,
this whirlpool of amphibious dreams,
has me caught in its loop - tight,
like a bug
on the windscreen
of the sandman's ride.
Through sweat drizzled skin
my whimpering heart paces,
as I keep waking – screaming.
All these different scenes,
uniquely distinct themes,
but always one constant - that face.
Always the last thing I see before I wake,
tears on my face forming a tremulous stream.

And worse.
When I wake
her eyes still burn.
Deep in my mind I see them,
combing through my memory room.
My store cupboard of old stories,
where fears and hopes loom,
like giant monoliths to some ancient god.
I see her wondering through the tombs,
where old loves, past friendships,
dead stories and more
are kept under lock and key.
Stored for posterity.

I haven't seen her in quite some time.
The one whose name
shouldn't ever be whispered,
for she whisks away your creativity,
makes your imagination
pull on its shoes and flee.
Talks inspiration into visiting
other people's dreams.
Leaving you asleep
in a dead seabed.
A salt desert,
assaulting the thoughts
that run dry through your head.

Left dying.

Empty.

Dead.

Just beware if you see that stare,
glaring at you
through swirly dream air.
Look away
as quick as you can.
Don't pay attention,
she only survives on fear.

Nowhere stare

I wear
my nowhere stare.
Seemingly unaware.
Distant
under people's glare.

I wear
my invisibility
like a coat of midnight.
I wear the sea of tranquillity
around my neck. A scarf tied too tight.

Always here,
but never...
there.

I wear a mask
painted with fear.

I wear my skin...   Hidden.
I wear my smile... Bitten.
I wear my love...   Smitten.
I wear...   *Listen...*

If anyone has taught me anything
it's to listen to the sound
that appears when your
thread is worn thin.
When the din in your
head is echoing. Begging
to be heard.
It's trying to sing
because it knows
what is coming.

And as you layer up
ready for what comes next.
Remember this.

The hum exists.

It picks you off
when you're at a low ebb.
It lives in the vibrations
of unsettled air, like a spider on a web.
Swirling through your head.
Where fear is emitted,
like a siren to lure it there.
It fills you with dread.
A sense of heightened trepidation.
So thick you could cut it,
like oven baked bread.

The fear is real.
The beast is not one
to make a deal.
So, take on a nowhere stare.
Look into the distance,
to a place that is not quite there,
but also nowhere near,
definitely not here.
Where perception of the ordinary twists
into a world more murky.

And take my hand.
Keep a tight hold of the thread,
connecting these twin lands,
keep that song spinning.
Drown the noise before it infiltrates your head,
or the hum will hunt you down
and make you wish that you were dead.

A leaf floats by

Glistening reflections
over granite pathways.
Blue lights dancing,
through the red stain
that remains where
the boy was slain.
It would be so easy
to let the energy drain.
To feel the pain
wash me away.

Down in the gutter
a leaf floats, *a boat asway*,
with all the other trash
that scatters over these streets.
It floats away.
A gang running away in the breeze.
When you have music and words,
love inside. You find a way to deal
with the worst of this awful
winter freeze.

My eyes glaze with frozen tears.
I see ghosts sway between the distant leers,
of the people on the stationary walkway,
this conveyor belt to nowhere.

I hear,
Hate
Licking
Serpent
Lips
listening to reptile minds.
Fear makes hate a friend of time,
but hate is *no* friend of mine.

With words flowing
through your soul,
love and hope grow,
not seeds of hate sown
into the slime
that is starting to glow.

In the shades, the hazy zones
where your vision fades.
Screams echo in your bones.
I see gangs. I hear them taunting
anyone they can,
anyone that won't stand tall.
Acting the big man,
when you are nothing
but a scared little boy.
I tune out the grind,
listen to the songs in my mind.
It's the only way to cope, I find.

In the glistening
raindrop reflections,
I see the glint of a knife.
Another lost to street life,
where your worth is shown
in how low you can go.
In how many fatal blows
you can bestow.
I pick up the sharpest tool
I can find.
My pen
and I write
it all
down again.

House of cards

There is rot
in the walls.
This crumbling
house of cards
should fall.
Towers of power
corrupt
with the stench
of stagnant lies.
A sewer
ready to erupt
before your eyes.

There is damp
in the walls.
This house
has seen it all.
Murderous treachery,
thieving
and lechery.
These leaders
should do a stretch,
for their parts
in this travesty.

The ground is stained
with dried blood.
Those who tried to be good.
Decent folks' bitter tears
soaked into
tarnished wood
over countless,
heartless years.

Ruled over by rats
and cheats,
lice and beasts.
Creatures out
to fill their lairs
with all that glitters.
They have no cares
these beastly critters.

The walls are
full of holes,
lies told
like sieves
trying to hold
onto an ocean.
They just flow out
into the open,
but innocent ears
and decent eyes
are blinded by
the lights so bright,
deafened by the lies
told by the vampiric parasites.
They hold out
their own throats
in their hands.
Asking the beasts
to suck them dry.

A world devoid of gravity

Misery loves the lonely.
It likes to keep you
contained.
Never entertained.
Trapped within your own thoughts,
in the quiet reaches
of your reclusive brain.
It wants to sit in the rain and play
solitaire with your mind,
but it likes to hide some cards
so, you can never win,
no matter how many times you try.
Just so it can hear
your silent,
whimpered cry.

Misery likes
the introverted.
Company is not
it's friend.
It wants you to feel
deserted on
your travels.
It wants to unravel
the unkind things
you think.
Just to see
what it can find.
When you journey to the brink
of the darkest self-loathing
cliff of the mind.

Misery is
a backseat driver,
guiding you
to an island
of solitude.
A Sat Nav system,
taking you
to the deep dark blue.
Then deserting you.
With no map or clue,
no light to show where to go.
A diver leading you
further down,
to places unfathomable.
Just you and the darkness.
Don't scream or you will drown.

Misery drops you
like a coin into a well.
To make wishes
for countless, vacant shells.
To fill with mindless
empty irrationality.
Breeding an army.
Just to become
another of it's
endless casualties.
Trying to find meaning
in a world devoid of gravity,
like biting on tin foil with
a mouth full of cavities.

A lost generation of one

I think to myself,
I'm in my own
lost generation.
A personal prison,
where everyone
is from a different time to me.
I'm lost in pages of history,
when everyone else
is in a future world of fantasy,
living incomprehensible
lives to me.

I don't know
the celebrity references.
The music preferences
are not representative
of the world
I once knew.

I don't recognise images.
Faces, I can't place.
I appear distant
to the people I meet,
when all I want,
is to welcome them
with open arms to greet.
It's like I'm from
a different century.
All that seems the same
is the hate that navigates
these unfamiliar streets.

Did I prick my finger
and doze off,
as a forest of change
grew around me,
like sleeping beauty
awakening in a world
from a deep slumber.
Surrounded by unknowns,
brain feeling dumber.
Mind turned to stone.

If I was a time traveller,
unravelling ancient mysteries,
this is how I'd feel.
Part of history,
but also startled and distant,
lost and alone.
Supposedly, this reality is home,
and I've been here all along.
So how is it, I don't know the songs.
The TV shows and movies
of which you speak
mean nothing to me.
Where was I when these things
became the norm?
Was I locked up in my own brain
just trying to conform?

Blood money

Does your platinum card
bring diamond dreams?
Luxury silk sheets, do they
keep the demons at bay?
Does all the champagne
ease the hurt of your painful campaigns?
Does it silence the echoes of death
that must sing like a choir through your brain?

How can you sleep?
Does it not build up?
The guilt, the death,
the lives that you take.
Don't you sometimes silently weep?
Knowing that the money in your hand
is the finger on a trigger,
and some poor soul's mother
is going to sleep having buried
a son or daughter. Doesn't it linger
long into the night?
The way your path
led to innocent slaughter.
Devouring any hope
of sleep you had.

How can you hide away
from the guilt inside?
Does your bank account
with all of its zeroes
make you feel like a hero?
You're no hero.
Death creeps through your blood.
Hate seeps through
the pores of your skin.
Ice flows slowly within.

Does your blank cheque
buy out the regret?
Bury the neglect
under 6 foot of gold.
No need for a soul
where you are going, I'm told.
Wealth beyond most
people's imaginations,
will it bring you salvation?
Blood seeps through the coins and notes.
Death lingers over every stone.

Selling arms
to slaughter innocent.
Selling death,
how can you dream
whilst hearing their final breaths,
their pleaful screams?
How can you sleep
knowing that your machines
are soaking generations in agony?
Creating seas of blood
for future children
to swim through.

How can you
look in a mirror
and not see the devil
staring back at you?

For just a second

For just a second
your eyes delved deep.
They caught mine,
and reached inside.
Twisted my heart
through my optic nerve.
I was held in place.
Tether tied to my seat.
A lead weight in my chest,
where my feathery heart should be.
Lungs forgetting
how to breathe.
I couldn't die,
I'd never know
how to leave.

For just the time
it takes for a butterfly's
wing to beat,
less time
than it takes
for a clock hand to creak
forward one tick.
Our eyes locked,
like how I image
our dreams to connect.
No way to pick the lock,
no key to untick the tock.
I felt sick.

My eyes had betrayed
my thoughts,
aired them for all to see.

Stuck still to my sticky seat
like glue had been poured over it.
I felt a click.
An instant of recognition,
you noticed my position.
I swear you saw my sweat glisten.
All I could do was listen
to my hearts pounding rhythm,
as it tried to escape its ribcage prison.
With painful precision, you glanced.
Enough to entrance.
I felt my blood rush my face,
an army trying to flood me.
I sat still, quietly in place.

Waving away wisps of fear,
I floated through the atmosphere.
Catching hold of my stray thoughts,
as they bounded
through clouds of long held doubt.
Too loud, I thought. Too loud
like they were screaming
from agonised lungs.

I let the winds take me.
On the wings of a song,
or the air of a memory
into a land of make belief.
Where dreams sometimes
come true,
I dreamed about you
and hope lives on,

Ever darkening shadows

These smoggy streets.
Gas lanterns burning,
cutting through
the darkness
a few feet
either way.
Slicing chunks
of the night
and throwing them
to keep
the wolves at bay.
Hope withers.
Shaking,
before fading in
with the grey.

She worked the night.
In the grimmest times.
These alleys,
her workplace.
Feet sore, blistered.
Haggard face.
She stumbled.
He quietly walked
like a shadow
in the soiled snow.
Trudging, she hears through fear pricked ears.
The dragged heels, picking up pace,
his heavy cane pounding a heartbeat
steadily on the ground.
He was just behind.
Nowhere to run,
no way her feet could drag her
away from here.
Away from hell.

For this was to be
her last night,
and on that
cold paving slab,
she saw dead eyes
staring back.
A man,
the media had named Jack.
Surgical gown
stained in lives,
started his attack.
The gaslight dripped red.
Her screams
unanswered.
The night fell quiet
her screams
went dead.

Ten bells,
only a stone's throw away
from where Mary Jane Kelly
walked into that foggy haze,
but no one
will see her here again.
Not today,
nor any day.
Her body lay where it was slain.
The red stain will never wash away.
Remaining throughout history.
A memory on Whitechapel's collective brain.

Jack sits and drinks,
thirsty work he thinks.
As he downs another. 5 in a row
and the police will never know.
He walks off
into the ever-darkening shadows.

The dead space in my head

I walk past the old cemetery,
the dead space in my head.
Searching in vain
for a place to quieten
the constant rain.
Looking for a piece of life,
to find some
peace of mind.
To piece together
this jigsaw-puzzle brain.
It's a hard place to live sometimes.
It's always so constant.
The noise.
It rattles away at all hours,
looking for cause,
looking for reason,
for purpose.
Sometimes I need to just search
for a place to bathe in still waters.

It struggles. On a page it can relate
tales aplenty. Make words settle like a sedate lake,
spanning whole land stretches.
All created in the briefest of times,
with just a flick of a switch.
But when it's in human company
it shuts down completely.
Leaves me naked, not wearing a stitch.
It seems to want to hide from day.
Leaving me to work
on emergency power, sparks ebbing away.
Everything is slow,
the words won't flow,
thoughts stuck, lodged tightly in my throat,
I stand exposed.

Anxiety leaks from the ceiling
onto me. *Into me,*
and I'm there standing
freezing. Stuttering
like a video buffering.
Waiting for the next piece to download,
before starting to play.
So, I just sway,
wobble and stare into space.
Trying not to overload.
People see me and walk away.
I'm a social person,
but I can't be social on cue.
It needs to be a connection
that feels true.
It takes time to grow.
So, for those moments
the vision of me seems a little askew.

I wish I could be like you.
I'd love to walk into a room,
be able to share,
be less self-aware.
I'd love to be able to speak,
to be able to joke,
like I do when I'm with one
that I can open up to.
But in a room.
I feel encircled.
My thoughts unravel,
just waiting
for the ground
to open up
and swallow
the thoughts
that spiral.

Velvet cushion of dreams

Could you be the one
I've been thinking of?
Dreaming of.
Could it be you?
Are you the one
that makes smiles bloom
through the pain?
A flower in a field of weeds,
are you the steady rain?
Soothing the heat
when anxiety makes
the blood rush to my face.

Are you the one
of which I think
when night falls?
Do your words
flow on the jetstream?
Is it you
that comes to me?
When the liquid night
is a river rapid
not a stream.
When the waters
are frothing,
bubbling.
Is it you
that tells me
to welcome
the moonbeams?
Walk on the
velvet cushion of dreams.

And is it you
that says
it will be okay?
When the fear
starts to rise.
Is it you
with the stardust
in your eyes?
The universe
in your smile.
And will the sun
still light my skies
if your voice
is no longer there?

Sleepwalk into a daydream

Don't want to sleepwalk
into a battle
that isn't worth
fighting for.
If hearts were drawn,
would loves blood pour?
Are we sure
that this is what
our dreams
are pointing towards?
If yes, then we
should run forwards.

You see, I let myself
get attached to a daydream,
then watched as it flew
into the arms of another day.
I let thoughts of happiness
silence the alarm bells scream,
as I let my hope
guide the way.

I let myself get carried
on a tidal surge.
Emotion: I let it envelop me.
As it grew
the fear
I should have listened to,
floated away.
I swam headfirst
into an illusion,
swept along on
waves of confusion.

I drank from
a river of lies.
I took a sip from
the waters rapid flow.
To my surprise
the taste was nice
but the sickness inside
gnaws and grows.
I don't want to feel that pain,
don't want to swim
where that river goes.

I flew in clouds,
dodging thunderbolts
aimed at the heart.
I dug in the dirt to fortify
my targeted life support.
I let the battle rage overhead,
as I silently lay there playing dead.
Praying for rain
to wash away internal stains.

So, I don't want to stare down
that barrel again.
If love is not real
don't aim
to bring me pain,
but if your heart
beats true,
I'd take
a bullet for you.
If we sleepwalk
in daydreams together,
then let's make
them last forever.

Watching through closed eyes

We watch our dreams
through
closed eyes.
In darkened rooms,
under nightmare skies.
We listen
to the sounds. *Still.*
Echoing eerily.
Filling
your mind's eye
with visions,
that come
from nowhere,
then fade
into the ether
just as fast.

Snippets, movies, ghosts.
Phantoms taking home
in your heads whilst you lay
at your lowest,
most defenceless.
Walls lying on the floor,
crumbled off when you
poured out of your clothes.
Now you lay vulnerable
to any ghouls
that wish to play.
Pray for the watchman,
or for them
to all stay away.

We see these visions
in those
sleepy hours.
When we are
veiled in darkness,
in a blanket of despair.
When the chill in the air
isn't the cold wind,
or snow falling on the streets,
but an invisible hand
tugging
at your sheets.

Because sometimes
these dreams
are not dreams...
They don't only become visible
when our eyes are closed.
Whilst we doze.
They are not dragged in
by sheep leaping.
Sometimes there are
beings creeping.
Just out of your line of sight,

To the right.

No wait.

The left.

It's behind you now.

That cold, cold breath...

Unfinished

When social life wipes me out
and quiet time is needed to thrive.
I find a dark corner of my mind
and sit. Letting thoughts unwind.
It's hard sometimes
to shut out the noise.
The grind comes
in annoying chorus.
A sea of voices,
all coursing over me.
I end up shipwrecked
on an island,
in some long distant
fantasy.
Surrounded by forests
of never-ending trees.

I scratch away
at the tree bark in my mind.
Etching out the thoughts I find,
the witty lines,
the silly rhymes,
the deep soul searching
treasure left hidden behind.
On this island paradise.
I sit.
Surrounded by
a forest of words.
All the poet trees
you see grown
from tiny little seeds.

But sometimes
I'm just trapped.
My mind blocked
like a drain
filled to the top,
and the water
keeps coming.
It won't stop,
but it has nowhere to go.
So, it just overflows,
painting the ground below.
Soaking into the roots
helping the trees
to grow,
but I'm left tired,
worn out.
I'm left with
A brain that feels
diminished,
and so many
poems
that just go unfini

The gaps between minutes

The slow ticking hands
creep achingly past.
Casting glancing shadows
over the vast gaps
of the weathered face.
The creaking sound,
gasping for air.
Clicks as it
snaps into place.

The sedate ticking hands
creep through
the misty gloom that looms,
towers over you.
In those cavernous spaces
that consume the gaps
between minutes, between hours.
Whilst forever
is catching up
and someday is only
a short breath away.
Somewhere
in the distance.

Those big empty
spaces on the face,
filled with shadows
of impending seconds.
Minutes away the hours start again.
Never ending.
Ticking to their own steady rhythm.
But here in this little pocket universe
time seems to be nothing
but a short verse, repeated into infinity.

The steady groan,
as the hands roam
over that empty expanse,
where near and far
meet in equilibrium.
Where they dance.
to the awful grind.
The clicks remind
that the second hand
never sticks,
and the ticks and tocks
will follow quick.

That worm of self-doubt

That worm of self-doubt
digs itself
right through
my brain.
Chewing up
my thoughts
and spitting out
negatives again.
The shopping bag I carry,
declaring
every little helps,
overflowing
with questions,
unanswered yelps.

My anxiety holds
on tightly to me.
Clinging for dear life.
He knows
if I let him fall
he will fade
into nothing at all.
He talks to me nightly.
I am in fright you see,
not of flighty fiends
but of my own torn dreams.
The ones that only
make sense at the seams.
Am I doing this right?
Is this train
of thought
the right one
to alight?

The flittering doubt now flies
around my chest.
Tickling my heart,
making it skip beats in protest.
Though the heart beats harder
to keep itself alive.
Sharing its love far and wide.
My doubt climbs up my spine.
Now with jittery insect feet,
it changes all the time.
It makes my limbs
feel shivery and weak.
It reaches my vocal cords,
makes it harder to speak
but I force the air through.
It's all I can do.
Make my words sing
to all of you.

Radium girls

Didn't know any better.
Didn't know any better,
and as the tears fall wetter,
the innocent bleed.

It's funny how the need
for innocent blood
always seems
to feed the greed.

They thought life would glow.
Radium girls beamed.
Riches flowed
wherever they chose to go.
A dream.
complete with its own light show.

Jaw ripped open,
crumbled fine dust.
Jugular vein rains
red spray through
gurgled breath,
like a drainpipe
started to rust. Collapse,
and death
had them firmly
in his skeletal grasp.

Didn't know any better.
The blisters swell.
Didn't know any better,
but their bosses knew
only too well.

Radium girls.
Ghosts on the street.
Glowing in the night,
radiant shine to their teeth,
fine dust around their feet.

Radium girls.
Phantoms on the prowl.
Walking dead.
their screams would howl.
When the pain became
too much for their light heads.

Didn't know any better.
Didn't know any better.

As the body shredding, bloodletting
made the glow so much redder.
Their bosses hunched their shoulders,
lied, and said they never knew any better.

Haunted

Haunted.
Hunted.
When I'm alone the voices
shout.
Things keep flying about.
I lose the will to fight.

In fact, I lose everything
that isn't nailed tight.
Things keep floating,
flying.
I often hear
the painful sound of crying.

*Is it mine? It sounds
like the eternally dying.*

Haunted.
Taunting voices tease.
Can someone get me
out of here please?

*The atmosphere
is killing me.*

It's dead in here and I'm
down on my knees.
I'm going to lose
my will to fight.

I sit here for an entire night,
with just these ghouls for company.
Feels like eternity, only trying to cause
me fright. *Oh shit.*
Now they've turned out the light.

Haunted.
I'm surrounded
by vague figures,
faking transparency.
They are see-through,
but their thoughts
don't speak true.

They just want
to grind you down.
Sow the ashes
into the ground.
Tie your mind in knots
until a tangled mess
is all you've got.

These ghastly
wicked voices leer,
in the still
delicate air,
they speak.
It crackles
and creaks.
Ready to splinter
into your hair.
Filling your heart
with despair and fear.

Polly Peggs

Polly Peggs plunged into icy water,
saw her life swim out before her,
as she sunk into the depths.
Those final gasps,
those frozen breaths.
She saw herself, before.
Walking on the shore.
A long time ago,
when the darkness
didn't encroach and the cold
didn't grow bold and approach.

Deep in love, Polly Peggs did fall.
Those first blossoming
flowers started to spring.
Her heart truly did sing.
The enamoured song of a lovebird's call.
Until one thing
led to another
and so, it was she was due
to become a mother, but there was no ring.

Frightened, tried to hide but
the tell-tale signs burned bright
like a candle flame.
Alas her truth was found out.
Illegitimate. *Shame.*
Bringing a stain upon our name.
The blame game, every wicked name,
used to frame the girl for being human.
Made to stand in white penance shroud,
in front of the pious angry crowd.
All day and all night. Paraded before all.
Demonised, despised, derided
until she couldn't take any more.

Cold night, wintertime.
No daughter of mine.
Doors slammed shut for good.
Outside she fled. Alone, afraid.
Nowhere to run.
Voices in her head.
Shame. Shame. Shame.
No-one to turn to.
No-one to love her
the way they should.
Just those same voices again.
Shame. Shame. Shame.
She dived into the lake instead.

Polly Peggs threw herself to icy water.
For shame of an illegitimate son or daughter.
Bringing dishonour upon everyone.
What honour is a hurting daughter
left to fend alone?
When all she needed
was a comforting arm,
some love and hope.
Instead, they basically handed her the rope.

Such a shame, they shamed themselves,
by blaming this poor innocent soul.
Now when the moon sits full,
and dawn is birthing a new day.
They say she can be seen
crossing fields,
and disappearing into the depths.
You may even hear her weep.
if you see her by dawns early light
show some love to Polly Peggs.
Her one crime, falling in love
during the wrong times. A crime that took her life.

Sleep no more

Sleep no more,
for unto your dreams
the unruly demons
have poured.
The force of army's
from lands of fire.
The denizens of death
won't ever retire.
They are firing
their weapons
with passionate glee.
They keep sounding,
loud pounding
noises at me.
Blaring alarms
when the dreams
start to calm.
To bring forth the terror.
The wild ferocious storm.

Every person
asleep in their beds.
Is in their grips,
their clawed evil mitts,
the scraping sounds
they emit.
Shredding, grinding deep
into your heads.
The sound of death
to the already dead.
An unholy riot,
a disquiet so perverse
and disturbing that your thoughts
can no longer converse.

Where, oh where,
is the watchman?
Where is
the night's saviour?
The knight
of the moons
round table.
The one that will answer
our sleep deprived prayer.
Where is the watchman?
Doesn't he care?

He is in
the throes
of a dream.
A vision
so vicious
that his mind
is delirious.
If he survives,
his mind
will be twitching
and itching
for death.
Wanting to put
his guitar
to his head,
and ring out
the loudest chord
he can strum.
To stop the sound
of the marching feet
as they come.

Outsider

I've never really fit in.
An outsider
to every party within.
I was never popular.
My features
didn't fit your settings.
Easy to forget.
A starving creature,
just there to tease,
then send off begging.
With no food
on my plate
nor a bed to lay in.

The way I talked or didn't,
made me seem distant,
aloof, in truth I was scared.
I couldn't get my voice to raise
beyond a squeak.
You just took the micky when
It leaked out in mousy speech.
Making me a prime target to tease.
And my mind was different. *Difficult.*
Full of holes like Swiss cheese.
So, you would set me traps
to see the way my cheeks
would turn
fire extinguisher red,
as if to blend in
with the very thing
I would use to extinguish the fires
that burned in my head.

You picked
and kicked,
spat and hit.
Made me feel small.
A speck of dirt.
Nothing much at all.
From the Earth I'd crawled.
You pushed me against walls,
on the floor, to the ground.
Pounding fists knocking me down.
Just because
I wasn't like you.
Because I was singing
a different tune.
I was playing the backbeat
whilst you were the front man
acting a buffoon.

Now I walk
on these wobbly feet.
Painful soles, cramping heat.
Ripping tears out from my eyes.
But
I don't let the eyes of others
make me feel small.
I won't let the world grab me
and pull me into the dirt.
I won't wear a glass shard crown,
just for wanting to be myself.
I choose my own path,
and I chose the one
with less hurt.
The one
I'm already walking down.

Sheep in wolves clothing

Just a sheep
in wolves' clothes.
He walks
in lonely shadows,
as they stretch out
in front of him,
growing potent
like a bad omen.

Allows his smile to lift
for its allotted moment,
before its pulled screaming
from his dejected face.
Should be used to this
bitter aftertaste.
It never gets erased.

Loneliness
is all he sees
from sea to sea,
only one piece of land.
An island in the midst.
Just him statuesque in the mist.
Buried like
a cursed treasure
under sand
that never seems to end.

Can't see the horizon.
The way
the light bends
around mountains to avoid him.
Eyes tighten
from cold wind biting.
His bomb blast skies
never seem to brighten.

Lone wolf
draws out a howl.
Allows it to sit
in his worn throat.
No pack to call,
no one
to hear him growl.
He just ambles
along.
Wondering how his life
went so wrong.
Where the waters end
and the lands begin,
nothing makes
any sense to him.
Thoughts are fogged,
eyes water-logged
like glasses
drenched
in tears.
The pain sears.

In the brief meanwhile of life...

You smile.
That knowing smile
and my legs fall out
from under,
but I'd still crawl the earth,
to be there,
in that
brief meanwhile of life.

The moments
that matter most,
are the ones
you don't notice at first.
That once
they are missing
from life,
make you feel
you must be cursed.

You look into my eyes.
An embrace
for the mind,
a dance of
souls entwined
in this frozen
second of time.
This brief
meanwhile of life.

And you smile.
That glowing smile
and my mind fails.
My once quick
mind. Slow
as a snail.
In this
brief meanwhile
of life.

And you speak.
A whisper
seeking my ears.
Inside it seeps,
a delicate
lingering
word of hope.
Love.
That word
so often
thrown around,
but not really
known about.
but in this
brief meanwhile of life,
of love
there is no doubt.

A storm in the loveless city

The rain
wastewater
floods gutters,
as he sighs.
Asking for the storm
to rip apart the sky.

In the deluge he feels
his emotions flood.
Endless love.
As his hands
reach out
to feel the
weight of rain
wash away
the pain of doubt.

He looks
into her eyes
and sees
a lightning strike,
glowing
like the seed
growing
a tree of sparks
that will set the heavens alight,
before the passionate
sounds echo.
Delight as delicate desire
ignites fires, devouring the skies
that burn so bright.

Electricity surges
through his blood,
and in that moment
he feels
the drips of rain tug
at his heart.
His thoughts flood.
He feels
the pull of gravity
dragging him
back to earth.
A moment of rebirth…
He feels
the mad rush of wind
fall to a stop. Drops to a still hush.
As the silence speaks
the sounds of love
over fields green and lush.

On his knees.
Worships
at the altar
of love.
Praying for the weather
to never change.
To keep bringing
her energy,
to share the storm
when she needs
to feed
on his electricity.
To wash away
the hurt
in this
loveless city.

Vermillion tears

There are splinters
over my reality.
Footprints
of miniscule insects,
crawling over
the fragile surface.
Their only purpose,
eating away at the strands.
Creating pathways
where their twitching feet land.
A web of scratch marks
clinging to worn skin.
Edged in darkness.
Head in my hands.

There are scratches, lacerations
on the tarnished skin.
Scars, hidden
deep within.
Faded leftovers
of torn out yesterdays,
drafted on burnt out paper.
The tears
of a million trees,
mix with the vapour
of the vermillion tears,
that I set free.
Evaporating
into the ether,
creating clouds,
that rain down
salty misery
upon the
warped ground
beneath.

There are cracks
in the threads,
of the strands,
in the fine lines of reality.
Bedded in so deeply,
they let the unearthly seep within.
The otherworldly beings creep
seethingly in.
Deepening your terror filled dreams.
Until you want to let out
the loudest scream,
but reality is twisted.
The threads constricting
your throat
and not a single note
will rise from shredded lungs.
Not a welp, nor a song sung.
Just the inching darkness,
getting ever closer.

If it ever reaches us,
then our time here is done.

End time news

The world is on fire,
ashes flying all around.
Air raid sirens sound.
Burning ground.
People laying dying.
Lava sprays and spews.
Yet it barely makes
front page news.
As the land sinks
into the sea,
time for another
shitstorm tsunami.
People wail and flee
"Why didn't anyone warn me?"

People retreat, awaiting calamity.
Insanity in the water.
in the sea.
In the soot filled air.
In the land we walk
with feet burned bare.

End time news.
Headlines
to see through.
Articles
that feed lies,
instead of truth.
End time news.
Nothing to see here.
Nothing to lose.
Just keep on preaching
it's no use.

End time news.
Humanity is screwed.
Our fate skewed
unless we do
as they say.
Fall to our knees,
lick the boots clean,
see your own face gleaming back.
In front of their alters
worshiping greed and money.

End time news.
If you get the blues
Take some pills. Don't worry
if they also make you ill.
We have just the right medicine
to remedy the chills.
End time news.
We have some
weapons to use.
They are gathering dust,
so, it's only right
we light the fuse.
Give them purpose
before they rust.

End time news.
Our seas are dying in waves.
They can't sustain life.
The fish dying. Sucking polluted air
from the water they breathe.
All the plastic and oil we leave.
End time news.
It's all death and decay,
but it will sell papers
until our final day.

Broken Britain

The snows of despair fall.
Cold air and blanket death shawl.
The forecast gloomy. Economic cold wind
blows right through me.
Here in broken Britain it's eat or heat.
Nurses at food banks. Extra socks
to warm frozen feet. A warm room
or a plateful of gruel to consume.
Whilst faucets shed icicle tears,
fat cats grin ear to ear, all the way to the bank.

No deliveries for days. Strike action underway.
Can't go away, trains not running today.
Daily Mail are up in arms,
these strikers are causing our country harm.
Typical sleazy tory scum.
A den of iniquity, this private crime lords club.
Lying, gaslighting, pushing the blame upon anyone.
But themselves.
Where people are struggling to survive,
bigwigs worry more about their economy drive.

This is broken Britain. Unlevel playing field.
Them at the top, us unable to climb all the way up.
Tory heaven. Think our health service is a plaything.
Limbs for selling.
Have us fighting, screaming and yelling,
instead of standing hand in hand.
It's not the homeless or the unemployed.
It's not the strikers just trying to get
their hard-earned rewards.
It's the men in suits.
Stamping out our lights,
under their thick heavy boots.

This is broken Britain.
Not the immigrants just seeking safety,
but our leaders who don't seem to mind a little tragedy,
as long as it pays them handsomely.
The media circus has got to stop.
The clowns should be marched to the chop.
This is broken Britain. People freezing,
because rich men want just a bit more,
but there is never enough to help the poor.
Always enough to fight a war.
Always some in store
if tory cronies need their
bank accounts to soar.

This is broken Britain.
On our knees, exactly as they want us.
Begging pleas, laughed off by Etonian toffs,
as they skip off to their second homes.
Well heated one would assume…
Bring the strikes I say.
Let broken Britain unite today.
Let's hit these suits where it hurts.
In the pockets. Let them feel the shame
of scrabbling in the dirt.

Broken Britain is being dragged through the grime.
Where race is used to sell papers,
but dodgy dukes do no time.
But God forbid you stand up
and say that race hate isn't okay.
Dare to say you were treated unfairly.
They will turn the blame squarely
back on you, and if you are pushed to the brink,
they won't stop, just try to make you jump.
It makes you think, or at least it should.
There is nothing great about this place,
not even much that is good.

Fallen angel

Used to call her angel,
now she is
self-portrayed as enemy.
Demonic entity.
A plague to be avoided.
The logical voice within says
that this is all in her head,
but the crazed screams
she hears in her dreams
say otherwise.

Her worlds collide.
A backwards slide,
two steps forward
to be pushed back
to genesis again.
No hand to hold.
Tears roll. No Eden
just this hell on earth.

The sound in her head screamed.
A shrieking gale force wind.
Was she evil?
Had demons climbed within?
Was she in love with sin?
Had it gotten under her skin?
One too many downfalls.
No angels call,
no heavenly choirs sing.
She just stands
arms wide apart
welcoming
the rain.

Windswept hair.
Wind swept her
into the air.
She sailed
on the breeze up there.
As I was winded,
wheezing to breathe again.
Watching
the aching pain
of memories,
too painful to share,
becoming a blurred heartache.
The wind song
never seemed to care.

A star
takes flight,
for the first
and last time.
The sky
cries crimson raindrop
tears to guide her.
Washing
her pain away.
As she lay,
a fallen angel.
Never forgotten.
Not even for a day.

Tides of moonlight over waves of midnight

Listen to the tides of moonlight,
as waves of midnight
wash over shores of relaxed insight,
but beware.
Sometimes the clouds
start to crowd.
A noise that rocks
the heavens on high.
A sound crashes
the rocks so loud.
The sound of hope
gone to die.

The sound of nightmares.
Cracking. Splintered, itchy noise
creaks through your bones.
Through the floorboards.
Scratches at windowpanes
with sharpened claws.
Piercing screams,
that come from nowhere.
The rattlesnake tail in the air.
The sound of despair.

Listen to the late-night silence,
absorbed by the thudding
jar of hearts.
The sound of a lie.
A lullaby to lull you to die.
Listen to the creepy chants,
repeated, over and over by phantasms
of the lonely lost lover.
The sounds of broken hearts
shattered into a million tiny parts.

Hear the maniacal laughter
of your own thoughts.
An orchestra of madness,
trying to cause fright.

Turn on the light.

It screams.

Turn on the light.
See the face
that haunts
your dreams.

.

Hear the pained echo of eternal screams.

Hear the pained echo of eternal screams.

Hear the pained echo of eternal screams.

Then realise the screams
are your own
and your eyes are
crying streams
as you sit there
all alone.

Won't get you far

It doesn't make you a man.
Running around with a gang.
Acting big shows how small you are.
A blade won't get you far.
It doesn't earn you respect.
Just the derelict thoughts
of a worn-down brick,
something that would crumble
under a rumble of bad weather.
You have so much more to offer.
Look inside. Then look outside.
See how far and wide
the world spans.
You can make things happen,
if you pick up a book and
put down the weapon.

Seeking respect?
Make people give it.
Show them what you can do
when you use your brain
the way you are able to.
This world is already
overflowing with pain,
why add to that?
Go out and make it better
with a pen and a writing pad.
You have the tools
inside your skull,
you just need to use it for
something more
useful than settling scores.

The blade won't gift you
the world you want.
It may give you life,
only it will be spent
in a prison cell,
where you will wonder
where that life went.
Every time they
shut down the lights,
you will be visited
by memories
that will haunt
your dreams at night.
The blade is not the way
to escape hell.
It is not a way to find
inner peace.
It won't give you sanctuary,
just a life watching your back
for attack,
filled with anxiety.

An eye for an eye
are two eyes too many.
So, open your eyes
and see
that this is not the path
that you seek
and the world
isn't your enemy.

You don't speak for me

Dear Mr Politician,
you don't speak for me.
Your words
don't reflect the world I see.
Your views,
not the views of the many
that employ you to lead our country.
It seems like power corrupts,
you lose all direction
on the moral compass.
Until it is just all spin
and no lasting peaceful policy.

You are not leaders.
A leader would look at atrocity
and try to stop it,
take pity,
instead of playing
the blame games.
Say 'no more' instead
of saying 'go on then.'

Drop all your bombs.
Kill and maim.
Children?
Fair game.
Shame
is upon you,
and clouds all of us
in your name.

You think laws only apply
to those you deem beneath.
Immigrants, who just want safe space,
to create a life less filled with grief.
Too busy thinking of your income levels,
debauchery, tales of parties, and arms sales.
If it doesn't fill your pockets
then there isn't space for it.
Think laws don't count for you.
Don't get your way?
Just abuse the system,
make the laws fit your view.
Fuck you. What next?
Join a queue.
We offer deportations
to anyone that doesn't toe the line.
This is a sign.
A symbol of our decline,
when our voices are not heard,
or we are ridiculed and maligned.

You think it's okay to bomb schools,
hospitals, places deemed safe?
You think it's okay
for children to fill mass graves?
This sort of thinking is deranged.
How can any of you sleep?
When hate is seeped
so thickly in your brains.
Now the country can't agree with any views.
What next, we all lose?
Or you fall on your swords,
do the decent thing.
Call a new election,
let the people hear their voices ring.
Oh, but then the money would stop rolling in.

Staring into the eyes of eternity

If today was my last day
and the universe spoke, saying
the hands of your clock
are slowing, soon they will stop.
I'd not drop to my knees,
praying forgiveness.
I've always tried to give all of me.
As open and honest as I can be.
I'd not regret loves that fizzled out,
friendships that crumbled into dust.
I'd not look at myself in distrust.
I'd know that everything I've done
was to be the best I can.

If I was staring in the eyes of eternity,
I'd see myself trying to fit in.
I'd only regret that I couldn't be more.
That I always kept a barrier or a door
to keep me from getting close.
I'd look at the things I never said,
the times I let my heart break instead,
but I'd not look at the past
as something to be forgiven.
I've always tried to give
rather than to be given.
I'd rather love than hate,
and sometimes I've had to walk
a harsh pathway,
but that always
seemed the right way.

If today I met my destiny
and I was taken from this place,
to be a piece of earth's long history.
I'd not look back with tears
at my lack of financial reward,
I'd not feel loss
at any gold or silver
I could have stored.
I'll look at the times I laughed.
The love I enjoyed. The times I heard
an audience applaud.
I'd reminisce of kisses
in the pouring rain,
of days when I could walk
without pain.
I'd look at the times I spent,
not how *much* I spent.
I'd look at what
every part
of my life
meant.

Forgive my season of silence

Forgive my silence,
if my words don't come.
If one day the words won't fall.
Does fall scare me?
That call of autumn and gold.
If the leaves have their time to die,
then how, in the still winter cold,
can my words keep falling free?
So glum when a snowflake
is all that will come.
Is that all there is to hold
and why does it fall upon my tree?
What if my words shake
in coldness
and only a
single shard
does form
and fall from me?

Forgive my silence,
if the summer sun leaves me
with no words to describe
the heat I hold inside.
The fire that rages wide.
If no words will trickle
to describe
the delicate ripple
of a gentle rocking tide.
Know that those words
are waiting in line,
to come
when it is
the right time.

Forgive my silence,
if the spring
leaves
me flustered,
from all the new
flowers clustered.
The lives that come,
and those that go,
in those
spring clean showers
where so many thoughts flow.

My words will form
in time,
but right now
I'm taking in the scenery.
Smelling the scent
of this grand bouquet
you see in front of me.
I'm letting all of earth's wonder
fill my mind
with all new thoughts to ponder
and new words to find.

Call of the void

Have you ever heard
the call of the void?
l'appel du vide.
It plants a seed.
Just a snippet
of a thought,
but enough
to make any more
thoughts flow away
into the breeze.
The siren song
to endless seas.
The song
of deathly nights.
It sings in harmony
with the hum.
Trying to take your light,
sever your connection to life.
Cut you dry,
to wander lonely tides.

It whispers on the wind.
Whilst the hum
grinds you down.
It won't leave you alone,
it will find you in any town.
The void is speaking.
Listen. It demands your ears.
Commands you to hear.
To wilt like a flower
quivering in fear.

The call of the void.
Intrusive voices
speak to you.
Tell you to do
the last thing
you'll ever do.
They whisper
to jump,
when you are near
a high ledge.
They tell you fall. Free,
be with them instead.
The voices
lie deep inside.
The hum has
buried them
in your mind.

When driving
at night
and you
suddenly think,
I can swerve
into the traffic,
just a flick
of this tired wrist.
Or when stood
at a bus stop
and you catch yourself
stepping out
into a road full of cars,
ready to end your life.
This is the call of the void.
Tune out the sounds
before they tune you out.

Dealer in a business suit

Pharmaceutical parasites
jeopardise lives
from corporate towers
in the skies.
Feeding their greed
with innocent cries.
Drug dealers
in disguise,
selling their highs
during office hours.

These lowlifes
deal in addiction.
Pain is just a means
to aid their infliction.
Money saves them
from convictions.
Greed is
their jurisdiction.

Literal opium
to the masses.
It's okay though,
'We have VIP passes.'
Get them hooked
and look the other way.
Snorting hits,
'It wasn't us.
The addicts are
their own worst enemies.'
Shifting blame,
whilst the money rains
death, it's all just life anyway.

Lies and deceit,
suave suited creeps.
Wonder how
any of them sleep.
Do they believe
that they are aiding?
Not just wading
in the ill-gotten gains.
The pills shorting brains.
Till ringing
still claiming
it's all about easing pain.
Money papers over the cracks,
but headstones stack up
and will one day fall right back
upon you.

Then will you take
the pill you prescribed,
taste your own medicine,
and see it all
from the other side?

A natural disaster

In secret I cry.
Rivers kept inside,
whilst the day is bright.
Floods of emotion wave out,
unleashed when night
sits beside.
Trying to grab attention,
trying to pull
the oceans closer.
I wish
I could express
the liquid thoughts
that leak from me,
in words
more translucent
than misery.

In those hours,
I let winds rush forth.
I spill out
hurricanes of noise.
I let the walls
feel the force.
Nature can't compete,
when my hurt
is so complete,
It's a part of me.
I wish
the turbulent thoughts
could be expressed
in words
more tempestuous
than pain and distress.

In secret I rumble,
as my thoughts mumble.
Quivering earth-shattering shakes,
making walls crumble.
Pain exasperated
amid soul wrenching
earthquakes.
I wish
I could expand
my thoughts
in words
more seismic
than despair and anguish.

In secret I feel a fire take hold.
Raging through my core,
right into my soul. The flames cold
against my burning pain.
Nature can't hold a candle,
to the fierce way my mind
picks fault
with the little flames
it brings.
I wish
I could express
the raging thoughts
in words
more combustible
than hurt and agony.

Circling wings

The swoop
of wings,
haunting,
like
a guillotine
cutting
the day
in two.
Left askew.
As if
to ask you
to put it
all back
together
again.

Those
circling
wings,
Ready to
devour
any weakened flesh.
In the weekend
fresh air,
it has its
avian eyes on me.
The umbrella trees
won't protect
from
the fear
that rains
from the skies.

I see a sea
of silhouette shadows.
Those
swooping wings.
Sweeping, swishing
past me.
Talons glint
in the midday sun.
Trying
to slash me,
but then
a kindly
smile
sets my
heart alight.
Gives CPR
with loving eyes.
Sparks a bit of life
back into this corpse,
and the vultures
fade from
sight.

THREE

**War, just an excuse for hate
bloodshed and heartache
let's make peace our legacy**

Apocalypse in HD

The world
is screwed
and we have front row seats.
Hurt projected in full HD.
Distractions
from what
we need to see.
The destruction.
The pain.
This constant insanity.

The world
is askew
and we have the clearest view.
A cinema screen in
within a
darkened room.
Sat in tearful eerie silence,
to witness the gloom.
The fear.
The violence.
This incessant impending doom.

The world
is fucked.
We see it every day.
A countdown on display.
Blinking down
the time
until our
final judgement day.
Mushroom clouds are on the way.
Ice will melt, seas bubble.
Price of food starts to double.

The world
is being read
its last rites.
Gun violence
on the rise.
Pandemics
ending lives.
Hunger games or real life?
Those with power
see profits raise.
Whilst we sit
in food banks
tears trickling down our collective face
from our hurt mournful eyes.
We watch them give themselves praise
for breaking rules,
that they themselves
put in place.

The world
is fucked
and we have
front row seats,
but all
we will do
is watch it
play through
our high definition
TV screens.

Date with destiny

Running late
for my date
with destiny,
and tomorrow
has arrived way
too early.

If I could stave off
that meeting
for as long as possible, I would.
I want to keep feeling the tide,
this high of life.
I want to feel the thrills,
not the edge of a knife.

You knocked
three times,
maybe more.
Whilst I was away,
mind laying on distant shores.
I always kept
a tight bolt over the door.
You tried to call.
I won't ever answer.
I have too much to do.
My life only just advancing,
like a dancer
that has regained
the feeling in their feet
for the first time in years,
or a drummer
that has found their rhythm,
the beat in between their ears.

I hear the knock, knock, knocking.
Bone fingers rapping, tapping a rhythm
on my door like nails on a coffin.

Knock.

It repeats over and over.

Knock.

A grating sound penetrating my mind.

Knock.

I can't escape the dreaded sound.

Knock.

Now it has lost its shock.

I expect every beat,

but I remain steadfastly in my seat.

You knocked so much,
your fingers must
have ground into bone dust.
You knocked so often,
the fear had gotten
replaced by boredom.
So, I stayed. I won't be leaving
until my time is outplayed.
I have so much more to do,
so much more to say.
So, keep knocking.
I won't answer
until my judgement day.

The intense silence

Through the silence.
Still. Solid. Silence.
Time has ceased.
There was once a hum.
The sound of a billion bees.
A buzz. But that has been
and gone. Now the air is dead.
Something is wrong.

This is somehow worse.
The atmosphere looms.
Oppressive,
breaths consumed
feel like fire
in lungs of ice.

Until now
There has always been
a background sound. A backbeat
to the orchestra of life.
So now that it is not around,
the world feels like it has
flipped upside down,
like living in a soundproofed room.
Even the voice you speak
stops at your lips,
drops silently to your feet,
gasping, quiet muffled cries,
before it gives in
and soundlessly dies.

The splinters across reality
have cracked
into whole chasms,
allowing an entity to suck out
our hopes and dreams.
Our sing song fantasies.
Our life signs that flowed
like sailboats
through our bloodstreams,
now aimlessly drifting
on an endless ocean
with no land to call home,
and no oars to row.

The silence
had started low,
but now it is
starting to grow.
Whole villages devoured,
no speech, no sounds,
just lifeless zombies
marching around.

Bullets and bombs

Bullets
and bombs.
The march goes on
across towns and cities.
A rhythmic thrum.
Drumming out
our final hours of time,
like a machine gun
shattering a clockface
until the hands have dropped off
and bells no longer chime.

Blood spills,
innocent kills.
Air raid sirens
against the still
morning frost.
The mourning.
Counting the cost.
Bullets and bombs
always seems
the way.
Bullies in arms
with their deadly
bullet spray.

Guns drawn.
Flags torn.
*Bodies litter
the crowded floor.*
Blood soaks pavements.
Can we end this call for war?
Bullets and bombs
will never win.
Always have to end up talking.

Buildings
crashing.
No doves
being released.
Missiles
smashing.
Where are the calls for peace?
Anger rising.
No talking.
Just hatred
in its most
hurtful guise.
No compromising.
Just bombs
dropping death
from the skies.
No white
flags waving,
just bullets
blazing.

Bullets
and bombs.
Sullen faces look on.
Witness to catastrophe.
Their lives carry on,
but with each death.
A little more humanity is gone.

3am: Haunting thoughts

The haunting
thoughts
taunt you.
Unimpeded.
Not wanted.
Not needed.

They seek to make
you feel weak.
To debilitate you.
Eliminate
the fight within.
Make you give in.
Accept that this
is your fate.

They start to push images through
the cloudy thoughts that shade your view.
They show you ways
to end your pain.
Take your life, let go,
then seed the rain.
Not wanted,
not needed.
Conceding.

As the sounds work their way
through the lining of your brain.
Deep inside.
Where they set up home,
twitching to life
and filling you with the noise
again and again.

It's hard to tune out
that sound,
to push it down.
To ground
yourself in reality.
It's like the aching scream of a stormy sea,
crashing at your exposed brain,
like a sea wall.
Not wanted,
not needed.
Depleted.

You feel your defences fall.
Letting the thoughts
infiltrate your core.
It becomes harder
to think happy thoughts,
harder to think at all,
as your body sinks to the floor.

Fight daily to not
let this parasitic
thought win.
Don't listen
to the song it sings.
Don't let it cling too tightly
to your skin,
searching for any pore
to climb its way in.
Don't fall too soon,
hear the beat
of your heart.
Find your feet, a way to detune.
Listen to the songs of the stars and the moon.

I am no longer mine

Starting anew.
Not going to
spend another day
thinking of you.
I say to myself,
knowing this to be untrue.
A lie to fill me with hope.
Instead of clinging to the past
like it's a dangling rope.

Not going to
turn around.
Not this time.
I say to myself.
Not going to
accept
the way you
make me feel.
How I can't
be seen
without your eyes
burning into my skull.
But I still
glance back.
Resist.
I must.
But temptation
twists
it's fingers around
my icy spine,
I am no longer mine.

Not going to look
in that rearview mirror.
Not going to
answer this call.
Not going to
let thoughts simmer,
I don't need
the downfall.
Not gonna spend
any more hours
thinking you had
some mystic powers,
that magically
kept me
trapped in your
locked up tower.
I'm not going to
give another breath,
to a feeling that
made me
feel like death.

Me, myself and the night only

Feels so lonely.
Me, myself
and the night only.
I look around
and all the people fade.
Disappear like water down a drain.
Blending into the roads,
just shadows or ghosts,
bending into the night-time hold.
It's so empty and cold.

I feel both closed in,
and like I'm standing
in a field with no ending.
My bed is like a grave,
duvet enshawling me.
Walls are closing,
and the ground is a hole
into which I'm falling,
but no one is calling me.
It's all so empty.

I stare out of the window
and all I see are ghosts.
Echoes floating
through the street.
Leaves on the breeze.
Leaves me cold.
All be told
if I could hold you here
I don't think I'd ever be able to let go.
It's so empty in this world,
without someone to share the view.

Ghost of the well

The ghost of the well speaks
in echoed song. Whispering,
of her final descent, sobbing
all the way down. A fall? No.
She was pushed by loves own
hands. Her heart was crushed,
as she felt the brushing slimy
stonework rush slickly past.
A trickle as her head, so brittle
hit the concrete at the foot
of this cavern so deep. Its
dimensions so little. A trickle
as the blood slowly leaks out.
A final view of the moon, as it
seeps into eyes that seek answers,
where answers will never be seen.

Eight fifteen on a Monday

Eight fifteen, sunbeams.
Hiroshima on a Monday.
Foreplay for the warmonger.
A quick fumble. Then it was over.
Mushrooms grow in nuclear glow.
Vaporised bodies.
Man's first taste of demons breath,
like dust blown grains of death.
Little boy in fiery demise.
Sky blooms and angels' cry
in the blink of a sunburnt eye.

The buzz of plane engines
Overhead. One look.
Then their world ended.
A blaze of anger and flame.
Warlike orgasm, mankind's shame.
Wonderstruck. A moment of pleasure
for those who adore pain.
then leave never to be seen again.

Manhattan project, desert heat madness
just because we can
doesn't mean we should.
Mushroom heads,
death bringers fingering the trigger.
An involuntary jerk. An evolutionary quirk.
Ringing storm surging through.
It feels so good.
Mankind loves to make people hurt.
The gasps of pleasure
as he applies the pressure.
Then release.
Fat man penetrates the clouds.

Eleven on that Nagasaki Thursday.
Mourning.
Howls of delight
as the instant
of madness, of pleasure
draws closer.
Pressure on the trigger.
Not a care
for people's plight.
No warning.
Blind to the threat, they swept
along on the waves of daylight.

A blinding light.
Fell to earth
under peaceful skies.
So many lost lives.
The screams of pleasure
in the desert many miles away,
could be felt reverberating
around the world,
and can still
be felt today.
Playing God
for a day,
humanities demon
for eternity.

A different shoreline, beside a different sea

My head
is so quiet.
I sit here
and nothing.
The words, unformed,
are not calling.
It's all so still,
like the sea
before a storm.
I know soon the wash
will pull me
deep into overspill,
into the deep currents. But right now
I sit.
Feelings, not concurrent,
like they are somewhere else entirely.

A different shoreline,
beside a different sea.

And then
I see your eyes.
I can't lie. I can't think.
I'm there in that space entranced.
Everything else
fades into the distance.
The way they speak
in so many unspoken words.
In unuttered tones.
I hear the rushing moans
of the waves crashing over me.

But my thoughts are still.
On a different shoreline,
beside a different sea.

As so often transpires,
I've been burning
more than candles at both ends,
but whole mental forest fires.
My thoughts descend,
like embers from high.
In-between the rushing traffic,
and the buses hassling for space.
In this station I sit encased.
I see your face,
for just a second,
it emblazons into place.

But my thoughts are still.
On a different shoreline,
beside a different sea.

But then I see your eyes.
It takes me a while
to breathe.
The way they smile.
The stories
hidden beneath,
like an ocean
that hides treasure
somewhere in the deep.
Everything else is weathered away,
just those stories and me.

But my thoughts are still
on a different shoreline,
beside a different sea.

The epitome of hate

Evil stalks the corridors of power.
A disease, festering. Unopposed.
It breeds, feeding on people who cower.
It leeches on insecurity, on difference,
It needs a suitable host...
Home Secretary?

Hatred. A fetid stench
that poisons the very air
we breathe. Play the blame game.
Blame anyone and anything
except your own inadequacy. Shame.
Cause division. Split the crowds,
herd the sheep-like people into prison towns.
Use the press, it's what it's for,
tell lies to cause uproar.
Instead of seeing you for what you are.
Peaceful protest - hatred.
Homelessness   - a lifestyle choice.
People choose to die to the elements?!
Shame on them, take away their tents.

The epitome of hate
isn't people walking
peacefully to state
that atrocities are not okay.
Hate is defending
bombing hospitals,
ambulances, children.
Wanting to cage the migrants,
lock them away.
Hate is punishing people
for wanting to live in a world
of peace. Hate is a disease
and patient zero is sat in tory seats.

Hate is
not batting an eye
as national front
marches by,
but frothing
at the mouth
when people of all
religions and faiths
come together
to march for peace.
Hate is a stain.
It grows and grows.
It starts as a smallest blot
but before you know
it's taken over your skin,
coated you from head to toe.

Maggie took milk from the
mouths of children.
Boris called covid
nature's way of dealing
with the old.
Now they want to steal tents
from the homeless,
and when they start
dying from the cold
claim it is right.
At least the jobseekers
will have a job for life.
Clearing the corpses,
treating people like rats.
Hate is the state
into which
this country is falling.

On the road to war

On the road to war,
end is getting close
'But what can we do?'
The words tinged in woes.
I hear you.
No angry cry. Just a whispered sigh,
accepting fate,
instead of screaming out loud
that this shit just isn't right.

We can raise our voices.
Let people know it's not right,
we have choices, put down our weapons,
when they ask us to fight.
I won't go quietly into that battle.
I'll go with both arms tied tight,
shouting that no war is just.
War is just not right.
Let's put mind over might
and hold our nerve tonight.

'What can we do,
I'm just an ordinary person
going about my life just like you?'
Well for starters,
don't accept the gun or knife.
Put down weapons, pick up pens to write.
Pick up paint and spread it out.
Grab a megaphone
and shout out loud.
Show the men in suits,
the people in high places,
That our billions won't bow
to their shameful status.
We won't take this.

On the road to war,
but who is the enemy?
Is it people living their lives,
or the suits and ties,
that will never get blood
on their white shirts,
will never see the fear
in a dead man's eyes.

'But what can we do?'

We can say no.

Stone stories seep into view

Lost in the creased pages
of a twisted nightmare.
Haunted house's diseased stare,
through grimy window eyes,
menacingly
disturbing lullabies
until they leap into the air.
I run through
deserted
overgrown cemeteries.
Morning dew soaking my shoes,
as the grass pierces through
the soil
like zombie's hands
reaching out for you,
clouded in low-lying mist
stories seep into view.

Horrifying hospitals.
Psychotic doctors,
as lightning flashes,
strobing, burning the eyes
in their sockets.
Thunder rumbles,
echoed groans.
Sky grumbles,
tortured moans.
Storms, wild
and crashing.
Devil's dancing evilly,
and me,
trying to
catch my breath.
Stolen away from me
by vicious fiends.

I'm lost in these pages.
A maze
of bewildering lines.
Words that lead to dead ends.
Exits that I can't find.
Worlds that I can't comprehend.
Too vast and complex.
All too many twisted signs,
passages that shift
through the mind.
Blending with the
linking thoughts
and tearing them
into confetti strands,
that now only flow
through my open hands.

The creepy details
derail the train
of my thoughts,
and I'm back once more.
In front of this haunted house,
complete with crooked door.
Strips of newspaper
plastering over the cracks.
Where, if you peer closely,
you see eyes
staring back,
and I'm lost
in the pages.
Seemingly no way
to escape.
So, I'll find
a safe space,
sit and write tales
of this place.

If I can't see them, they can't see me

So many
ghosts,
possessing
my memories.
Too many.
I am
speaking Latin
almost constantly.

***Poetry break*
Why do demons
only speak in Latin?
What did they do before,
just wander
aimlessly, depressed
unable to possess,
"Oh, however will we
possess thee?
Someone get me
a Latin to English dictionary"
End of poetry break***

So many ghosts.
They linger in my home.
Making my bones creak,
making me feel weary, sick and weak.
Only so much air in my lungs to shriek.
So instead, I shiver and shake,
quake in terror at what could await.
Pull up the duvet,

If I can't see them,

they can't see me.

These ghosts lurk,
irksome beings
that loom in the dark.
Just to feed me with words
I don't need to hear,
like my head is empty.
Yeah indeed.
As if I need
another set of voices
to talk amongst this
already crowded
night-time chorus.

The memories
stain every surface.
Ectoplasm.
Must be a phantasm,
trying to take advantage
of the aching
cavernous chasm,
that has
become vacant
in my head.
Look, can't you just fuck off.
I want to be asleep in my bed.
Take your chains and your sheets.
Your woo's and floorboard creaks,
and leave me be.
Go and haunt a tory instead.

Books, not bombs

Send books
not bombs.
Hugs outweigh
ammunition.
History
teaches lessons
to those
that listen.
Bad intentions.
cause rivers of blood
to glisten.

So, read
and don't repeat
the same frustrating
storylines
over and over.
Send love
not guns.
Hope not aggression.
Fighting just heightens
oppression.
Let us free minds
send a message.

*"We don't want
this never ending
cycle of death."*

Send handshakes,
not hand grenades.
Share landscapes,
instead of taking lands.
Pull down walls,
instead of building fortresses.
Stop looking with distrust
at all these people,
just
like us
All they want
is to live freely like you and me.

Send cuddles,
not cluster bombs.
Feed minds,
instead of
seeding minefields.
Send dreams
not nightmares.
Send goals,
instead of
planting your flag there.

Let's put behind us
this human curse
of thinking we own
any part of this earth.
Of thinking
that our borders
mean something.
They are just lines
drawn on a map.
it's all a trap.
To keep us blaming others
for our own inept government
and its warmonger crap.

Dream with me

Come and dream with me
of fields where we can walk.
No-one to bother us.
We can be free
to spend our day in bliss as we talk.
Kiss the words
that leak from your lips.
Take them in, like nectar,
sipped from fountains that never stop,
as we stroll along peaks,
weather beaten mountain tops.
I miss the days where I could
look into your eyes.
A longing gaze
dreaming of waves,
of waterfalls that embrace us
in their cooling sprays.

Come dream of tomorrow
and all the days to follow.
Where we can be within each other's arms,
our safety blankets against the cold.
Palms held together, as we watch our days unfold,
like a paper map
with gaps for us to paint our stories whole.

Dream with me,
of blinking lights over distant seas.
Shooting stars guide us together
to show where we need to be.
Fingers clasping tightly in all weathers,
never sever bonds that tie.
Our lives held tightly,
in our dreams we fly
hand in hand towards the star filled sky.

A breath

A breath.
Just a breath. It's all I ask.
I'm gasping, choking in here.
My thoughts are too tight.
Too much fear.
Constricting my throat
every day and night.
A breath of fresh air
would fit just nice.

A breath.
Just one single gulp.
A taste of that
citrus fresh oxygen,
not an air full of rancid pulp.
Into my lungs I'd pull it deep.
The anxiety has left me
worryingly deplete.
A breath of fresh air
would be right up my street.

A breath.
A taste of life
inhaled between
my scared cries.
I'd take it in. Give it home.
Let it roam across my lungs,
filling my blood with oxygen,
to feed these starving bones.
For the worry
has knocked the wind out of me.
A breath of fresh air
would suit me perfectly.

Kyle Coare

Not in my name

Not in my name.
We didn't vote for this.
We don't condone
this endless march to war.
It will be forever etched upon our tombstone.
A sea surge
of opposing voices,
sing a chorus,
yet you choose
not to listen to us.
Left or right, we lose.
All you want to do is fight.
We stand voiceless
in the sniper sights.

Not in my name.
Where is your shame?
Babies killed
and you
won't take blame.
Self-defence. In what sense
is killing innocents
a means to an end?
Selling your country,
our souls,
down the river,
for some extra
pocket change.
This thinking
is deranged.

Lay down your arms.
Sheep follow the clowns.
Bleat.
Sound the alarms.
War is coming
to town.
Put on your best suit.
Take to your bullet proof
bunker. Call on your troops.
Send them out on our streets.
Call on the poor.
Call on everyone.
Whilst you sit
behind bolted door.
Watching your
computer screen
as the obscene
blood money
comes pouring in.

Refuge

Refused refuge.
Distorting truths.
Stop the boats,
right wing news spews.
We are full
we don't want you.
Use terms like surge,
hurricane, swarms,
torrents, floods.
An act of nature
that will bring with it blood.
Political figures smirk with glee.
Division is a sure way
to keep people on their knees.
Breed fear in the populace,
they will beg you
to set them free.
Even though we
are the ones
holding the key.

Politicians take refuge
in their crumbling palace.
Phallic towers built on lies,
spite and malice.
Whilst the populace
seeks sanctuary
in the nearest
mind escape factory.
Anywhere they can be taken
away from their lives of drudgery, of mental
enslavement to a pack of jailers
who should never hold the key.

Refuge. To feel safe.
A haven from the fear
of life being taken away.
A fear of the state.
A shelter from the downpouring
slate like rain of terror,
that is always flooding their door.
Only to be called
criminals, opportunists, hordes
and barred entry
with a barricade of hate
from those who should offer love
but instead
instil people with
that primal urge
to want kill.
To see rivers of blood spill.

Life has no borders, those lines
are there to distort us, divide us
and cajole us into
our fenced in prisons.
We are one, a community of earth. A union
of souls with one goal. To live and thrive
but we get drip fed soundbite lies,
about them against us.
Haves against have nots.
Rich against poor.
Poor against poorer.
These words set fire
to the bad blood that pours.
So let us open our doors,
and offer refuge to help the cause.

Porcupine

Pull back
the bow,
let your arrows fly
into my skin.
They pierce
but I don't fall and die.
I stumble.
Struggle
to stay afoot
but I keep on walking,
mouth sewn shut.
I won't let
your poison darts
pollute my heart,
or cut me down.
I'll just
keep bleeding
all over
this town.

Let your arrows
pierce the air,
ripping wounds
in the
moonless sky
like blinking stars
crying out.
They penetrate
deep,
your arrows of doubt.
I feel my blood seep
but I don't fall and die.
I keep walking.
So, let your arrows fly.

I won't let
this pain win.
Just feel them
like a porcupine
with
prickly hairs
sticking out
of my skin.
Let your arrows
cut the night
in two.
They won't do
the job
you want
them to do.

I won't fall.
I'll keep
walking tall,
through the barrage,
as they rain,
staining the ground
with the contents
of my gushing veins,
but I've become
so used to it
I no longer
even feel the pain.

Headful of landmines

Troubled times.
I fill my head with landmines,
to stop the pain from drowning me
in a sea of doubt.
Troubled times.
Inciting violence on the streets,
in-fighting in opposition seats.
These seeds will soon grow
into a forest we can't
see or cut our way through.

Troubled times.
Electricity coursing
in the pouring rain.
I expose myself to pain
to stop the images
from shocking me.
Our shouts mean nothing
to deaf ears, they don't see signs.
They don't notice that
we've walked this road a thousand times
repeating again, the same old tired lines.

Troubles times.
So many tears cried. *Why?*
When we have the masses shouting.
What have you got to hide?
Do you enjoy inflicting pain?
Making the sky rain with fire again and again.
This is not justice. This is not just.
Is this what you want to tell your kids?
What you did, the blood spilt,
the innocent lives you undid.

Troubled times.
Pull your history books out.
Uncover your ears,
the drums are starting to pound.
I've seen this all play out over so many pages.
Across the ages. We used to listen to sages.
Now we just blot out the sounds.
Well soon the echoes
will be felt and not heard.
Deep inside we will die a little,
each life lost will hurt until
we are nothing but glass shards
cracked and brittle.

Troubled times.
Humanity should shine,
so why does it feel so dull, grim, and unkind?
Why do men have their fingers
on triggers so often?
Instead of sitting
in conversation.
It hurts to see so much pain
and to know that this is just another
history book beginning. Reality is thinning.
Blending, creating a new tomorrow,
and if we don't listen,
there will be stormy days to follow.

Count the cost

Count the cost.
A child's life,
priceless treasure. *Lost.*
Fired upon. *Gone.*
Count the cost.
Medics bled, *no guns.*
A bullet in the head.
Count the cost. Run.
Hospitals fled. *Buried dead.*
Once you see
all as enemy
You've already lost.

Count the lost.
Young mother.
Future unaccounted.
Encountered a sniper.
Enemy. Threat.
Heaven wept.
Count the cost.
Arming forces
that don't respect
laws. They have their own clause.
Once you start killing innocents
you get no applause. No rewards.
You're already a lost cause.

Count the lost.
All the blood.
All the limbs.
All the tears,
every drop spilling.
Count the cost.
Once you start killing
innocents you're already lost.

Count the costs.
Those that crash
down like rain
from above.
Follow the money,
watch who profits
from all of the blood.
Count the cost
of all of those rockets.
Count the cost
in feeding their pockets.
Once you start
killing innocents
You're all
lost.

Count the lost.
A generation,
and those left waiting,
will be left with hate
burned deep into their skin.
Living in fear of those
who brought forth this fate.
Count the cost.
Once you start
killing innocents
it's too late.
You've already lost.

All the roads down which I've walked

All the roads down which I've walked,
screaming from deep in my lungs.
All the storms to which I've talked,
all the songs the songbirds sung.
I wander under midday sun
and amble below midnight moon.
I wander on, wondering if this road
is it the right one.
Will I reach a destination?
Will it end soon?
An elevation above a river of reflected stars.
Will I see the eyes of the moon swoon
and buckle under weighed down hearts
or will that river just run and run?

All the ordeals, the travels, the trials
along unreal roads, so surreal, the miles.
I've tried to tiptoe through.
To be unseen.
Un-noticed,
but you noticed me.
You saw
the same forests I saw,
in those glimpses of dreams, of truth.
You saw, I'm sure,
the same sky I was looking on before.
When my
mind replays memories
and I think of that
one golden yesterday,
you see the same images.
So many galaxies away.
Where hearts once opened up
and together they played.

All the oceans
I've witnessed
crashing
before my
crying eyes.
The seas I've seen
smashing
against the
crumbling
shoreside.
You stood there watching.

Somewhere
in the sun's rays,
I sail through
in a floaty phase,
through the air,
I shimmer and fade.

The sea mist grabs
at memories
and swallows them whole.
In the haze.
the voice says,
walk on
and create
new memories
to replace.

Broken heartstrings

Two
different
songs,
completely
out of sync.
We spent so long
trying to make
the harmonies link,
when the whole soundscape
was being played
in a different key.
Where the lyrics
you sung
were not ones
written
on the page I see.

Our rhythm
was out of time,
yours beat so fast,
mine, slowly chimed.
Two songs played
simultaneously.
Each one a wonder
when heard individually,
but when
the sounds
blended together,
a cacophony,
played by a twisted
demonic orchestra.
A musical monstrosity.

Those heartstrings
were played,
on a harp
made of glass.
The shining light cast out,
dazzled and glared
across my eyes.
Blinding me to reality.
Twisting the image,
a window of fantasy,
and still the orchestra played.
Fingers frayed
by the razor strings
of the song set free.

All at sea

The debris
of sunken relationships,
drifts through
the oceans of my mind.
Currents of discontent
bubbling under the nervous,
rippling,
reflective mirror surface.
As I cling
to a piece of driftwood.
All at sea.
Just me.
Alone.
An island
in the open
ocean of love.
Faded into antiquity.

Driftwood bobbles under
waves of hurt,
as they spray over
my lifeless floating shell.
The rumble of water rushing,
the crushing pressure
of the depths.
As I sink.
Deeper
into the darkened lair
of the undersea creature.
I don't need to breathe.
This is all wrong.
I'm down deep,
and yet my lungs are full.
Not drowning,
nor screaming for air.

In this abyss
of lovelessness,
I try to swim.
Feet swing.
Arms pulling
the water around.
I don't know if I'm
going up or down.
Bubbles fill the water,
like disco lights
in a crowded club
on a Saturday night.
As I swim with all my might,
just to catch a glimpse
of the sunlight,
so, I can escape
my plight.

In these darkened depths I swim.
Velvet soft water against skin.
Makes me feel free again.
The fight to survive kicks in.
I thrash my legs,
running up a fluid stairway
towards the heights.
Beaming spotlight, ripples overhead,
scanning the surface of this inky graveyard.
Where ships lay broken and dead.
Only driftwood floats by.

I lift my head
and break through the mirror.
As the lifeboats
catch me in their light.
They throw a float to hold on to.
Another chance
at this thing called life.

Imposter syndrome

There is someone that lives
deep within my skin.
Ripping through when I'm subdued,
they let rivers of words flow in.
It's unreal sometimes,
the way they produce
worlds I can't imagine.
Places I can barely fathom.
They make words sing.
Whilst I struggle to even get
a sentence to begin.

They come when I'm drained.
When my energy has left.
When my will is sinking
they rearrange my thinking.
Filling the air with tuneful words
when my eyes start to droop
like a bird swooping down.
I know not where they come from
nor whether they will suddenly end,
but reality has started to blend
or maybe I'm morphing into him.
The words have started to come
from somewhere else within.

There is someone
that sits in my seat
when I'm asleep,
like a ghost or phantom
that walks
the night-time beat.
They take unfulfilled thoughts
and contort them, until the unformed
symbols mean something more uniform.

Have I been possessed?
Do I need an exorcist?
Or do I just accept this being
that takes over when I'm feeling
I'm no use. It seems to be trying
to show me the right path.
Maybe best to let it be.

As I become him,
he becomes me,
we become one,
a being of unity.
So, I let it
keep wearing me.
and see where
the words will lead.

Mist in the rain

In the overgrown church yard
a lone sunflower grows.
Bestowing an orange glow
upon the grey headstones,
left to fade in the rains
of so many unmarked days.
Names no longer visible,
just a barely discernible
stone silhouette,
amongst the grass forest
that towers around
the unkempt graves.

And the visitor

She sits, beside.

Weeping through foggy eyes.
Only noticeable
when the moon sits high.
When you turn your head to the side,
just a flicker of her faded figure
smears your mind.

A shift in the light,
you may think,
a trick of the mind.
A shadow forsaken,
but her face
cannot be mistaken.
She sits. Patient as a tree,
taking its time to grow high.
No rush, for it knows it will
one day reach the sky.

She sits.
Wishing to see him
once again,
but it's been centuries.
She has sat in this empty
churchyard cemetery,
and not a glimmer of his smile.
Not a shimmer of those kind eyes.
Just lonely, under so many changeable skies.

But

Tonight, the moon sees her,
and casts her light.
Slightly to the right.
Hitting the sunflower
to make it shine bright.
And there beside
the sunflower stands
a man. Waiting.
An eternity waiting.
The grey lady sees his eyes
but he doesn't see her yet.
The man shifts
his gaze just enough
for the light
to bring her into view.
After centuries
their story can resume.
His smile
outshines the moon.

They fade together

into the night.

Just mist in the rain.

Listen to the shells

When I was a child, we would play army.
Little did we know, that around the world
this was reality for so many young,
innocent minds. The sound of the war drum
was only a playground game. Not something
that could truly kill or maim.
Little did we know...
I listened to the shells
and all I'd hear were endless seas.

Those war drums seem to always be booming.
Tension is always looming,
when purse strings need fixing,
when popularity is taking a downward swing,
and those war drums really get the blood boiling.
They bring all the hate to the gates.
A different colour. *Hate, bomb them to the dark ages.*
A different race. *Not like us, castigate.*
Then blast away.
I listen to the shells
and all I hear are screams.

The war drums never stop.
Want to be free? *That isn't a choice.*
Want a voice? *We will drown it*
with ammunition noise. Slaughter,
poor innocent son or daughter.
Never chose to be surrounded
by the pounding war drum sounds.
Blame. If you pick a side. *Shame.*
You will be shot down in flames.
Even if the side you're on,
is the one that wants the weapons gone.
I listen to the shells
and I hear a world gone wrong.

Pushed from own lands. *Occupation force.*
Fish in a barrel. The pummelling begins.
War crimes sound the war drum grind
and the death bell chimes ring.
Think of the children they yell
but not those that are on the other side.
Hypocritical genocide.
Think of the women, but not those
that we starve, proclaim as enemy.

Cut the lights.

I listen to the shells
but all I hear is the endless night,
where all you can hear
are the drums sounding out.

Another rally cry,
those that oppose must die.
We have an itch to scratch.
Those whose skin doesn't match,
those whose beliefs don't fit with ours.
Divisions made. Land grab. Weapons raised,
and in the bombed playgrounds
of wreckage strewn schools, children dream
of peace. Two wrongs make twice as much
death go around, an eye for an eye,
leaves the image undefined.
Endless graves lay unfilled,
bodies lay under rubble undignified,
and the blood still spills
from those left unidentified.
I listen to the shells
and only hear more bad tides.

I see your scars

I see your scars. The way you keep
your sleeves rolled down. *Coving your arms.*
I see the smile that doesn't sit true.
It's in the lips but doesn't shine through.
The eyes you use to view,
see things from differing
perspectives to those around you,
this world so paralysed.

I see the slouched look
of defeat. As you stare at your feet,
moving between the cracks
on the paved street.
I see the way you keep people at bay.
Turn them away.
Keeping to yourself thinking,
it's better that way.

I see how you shy away,
hide in your mind palace every day.
Headphones on
to avoid the outside world.
I've seen you smile,
a true smile when the tune hits.
I've seen the way
you avoid eating,
even when your stomach
is aching deep in its pits.
The way you stumble to speak
then retreat back
to staring at your feet.
When you find the words
too difficult to reach.

I see how you grip
your phone,
always ready to focus
on the screen.
If you don't see them,
you can't be seen.
I've seen the way you
notice high places,
or how when there is
lots of traffic,
the briefest of dark thoughts
flashes
like a blinking light
across your eyes.
You could end it here,
but you know that
would be a terrible waste of a life.

I've seen all of these things,
because I've seen myself
in all of them.
In the mirror when I glance,
I've seen the scars
play out their dance
across my bare arms.
I've seen myself
clinging on to hope,
to avoid the hanging rope.
I've dug in
to not give in to the pain.
Even in the heaviest rains.
There is always
a chance of a brighter day.

Chasing ghosts

Feels like I've been
chasing ghosts for too long.
Those floating groans
echo through the solid foundations.
I've been listening
for the tell-tale haunting tone,
the one that whispers
when the ghosts are home.
The drone that spreads
through my head.
Remembering times
that are better left unsaid,
and times of spiritual enlightenment,
when the ghosts made me feel alive
when I should have felt dead.

Feels like all of my life
I've been chasing ghosts.
I walk, the same old bones,
the streets, the tormented stones.
I've been in haunted homes
and cemeteries.
I've heard their spectral moans.
Felt their weight,
pushing down on me
making it hard to scream.

Feels like I've been hunting
the haunting sounds
for so long I no longer
recognise the sound of this world
and its insatiable hunger.
Just the wails as they fill my ears
when the ghosts hail
to say come near.

Feels like I've been
seeking substance
in the silent
social society of ghostly life.
I've walked on the dark side,
and the light.
I've met demons and angels,
but the ghosts always
held me the closest.
Those phantom lips
the shear special blisses
of their spectral kiss,
before they fade,
into a vision unfocused.

Too much

It's getting too much.
Only so many tears
can rush,
before the pain makes
my face too sore
to touch, but I'd rather that pain,
than a world consumed by flames.
A pain so many children are enduring,
instead of enjoying playground games.

Warfare is unfair,
a cruel, bloody,
hateful affair,
and over there
people unleash
it daily
from the air.
Innocent children
left mourning
the death of innocence.

And we condone this,
say it is a rightful fight.
You have a right to defend,
but genocide is no defence.
There is no defence.
This is an offense
against
humanity.
We need to stand tall.
Our leaders need
to hear our call,
but they are too busy
trying to divide us all.

Media ties. Outright lies,
printed in black and white.
Paint victims
as aggressors.
Taint prisoners
as oppressors.
All the while
war crimes
are being ignored.
Phosphorus burns,
torn into children's bones.
Worried that some stones
may be thrown?
Or that you will be
knocked from your
gold plated throne?

So, our leaders condone,
whilst us, the people say
this is all wrong.
But they don't listen
to the masses.
When all is said and done
the only fight we should be having
is the battle for peace.
All gunfire and rockets need to cease.
Or *we* will become the monsters,
those mythical beasts.

Find me in the darkness

Will you find me
in the darkness?
Or come looking
in the shadows?
Will you see me
in faded silhouettes?
An outline of a man
out of time
with his own mind.
Will you notice
when the flickering streetlights
start glowing?
Lighting your pathway
more clearly.
When that harsh wind
stops blowing,
would you notice me,
holding the weather at bay?
To make your day
more comfortable,
less harmful in any way.

And if the lights all fade out.
I'll beckon the moon
to shine a beacon for you.
Making the pathway easier to roam.
So, you will always be able
to find your way back home.
But will you see me in the shadows,
hear me crying in the wind?
Will you know when I'm falling,
and how deeply I'm falling in?

And if life starts to crush,
I'll be there with a hand.
Ears to hear, a kind heart inside.
Just to help overcome
what may land at your door.
Never to take over, or push,
nor stand in your way.
Just to help if I may,
if it's what you want
you only have to say,
and I'll be there in a rush,
before the end of the day.

But if those shadows loom
too close to *me,*
will you shine your light
so, *I* can see?
Will you show me
that they are
just the dancing light
at play?
or would you
just laugh at me?
Letting me fear
my own
saddened screams,
my own demons
that sometimes haunt
my own worn-out dreams,
or would you
hold out a hand for me?

Robin our neighbourhoods

Like a back to front Robin Hood
stealing from the poor
to give the rich some more.
Up to no good in our broken neighbourhoods.
First, they said it was
about our health.
More like
a transference of wealth,
from the have nots
to the already
have lots.

It's a system
that is inherently flawed.
You are
asking greedy people
to forget their
instinct to hoard.
Wealth is meant to trickle
to those down below,
but those above invest
in bigger bowls
to catch the overflow.

Blaming it on a war now.
Missiles don't grow on trees
and we need these
to bring our enemies
to their knees.
Funny then how
it's us bowing down,
begging for scraps, cap in hand,
whilst money burns
along with innocent lives in distant lands.

Pound takes a nosedive.
Prices continue to rise,
until we can't survive.
Where is the anger,
the sense of injustice?
Have we all
become puppets,
working to fill
their pockets?

Seems like
the whole system
is broken.
Money, nothing
but a class token.
Profits soar,
but still, we must pay more.
Energy bosses,
record breaking profits.
Yet all we feel are losses.
Heating isn't a luxury
when we hit a deep freeze,
having food on the table
is a necessity.
So please,
give us bread
not austerity.

The killing fields

Hear the call up.
It will be fun.
A good war
never hurt anyone.
There is nothing more glorious
than battling for your land.
It's your duty son.
King and country demands.
Go on, sign on the line,
all your friends will be there,
it will be just fine.
It will make you a man.
Peer pressure. Stress invader.
The killing fields
are getting nearer.
You have nothing to fear.
The drums will be pounding
the sound of mortars in your ears.

Heed the call up,
it won't happen soon
but when it does
it will be played repeatedly.
Fed by drip feed,
over your mass media TV screens.
no silver spoon needed.
All over your social media feeds
people seeding the killing fields.
Led astray by lies and deceit.
As if the government
would send us to our deaths. Please!
Fear the call up, feed the killing fields.
Flowers grown from blood-soaked seeds.
It's near. Time is getting close. Mobilise
Sing songs as you march in line. Don't fear.
Patriotism drummed deep.

Propaganda mind control. If you say no,
ridicule will make you appear small.
School kids led astray. To fire guns
as if they are at play,
and in those killing fields
where they lay,
there will be no one left to pray.

Marching merrily into the mixer we will go.
The meat grinder will overflow.
Slops will drain over the fields below.
Another day, another time. Another war crime.
Led to the grinder like cattle to slaughter.
Let's silence the hate, you sons and daughters.
Shout as loud as you can.
We won't be part of this murderous masterplan.
We don't fear what lies in wait.
The killing fields will stay green.
No more blood will soak the soil beneath.
Stop the mass production of means of murder.
No more letting them get their way.
Let's stand as one and stop this, before it's all too late.

I will always refuse to fight.
Push me down, kick and bite.
Make me seem small, I'll take it all.
I'll welcome the respite. Lash me, beat me,
I'll still stand tall with my hands behind my back.
My words will do the fighting.
Angry gun chamber biting
against my head,
Feel the trigger. Pull it.
I'll feed your hateful, hungry bullet.
But I'll rise. My words won't die
and the killing fields will never thrive.

On the other side of Eden

On the other side of Eden,
no paradise awaits.
Beyond the gates
just an empty desert
bakes.
No oasis
in the haze,
just the
rays of sun
blinding
my gaze.
Just outside Eden,
and I turn up
too late.

On the other side of Eden,
they are feeding
on the lush fruits
from verdant forests
of vibrant trees.
Feasting
on all the wonders
life bequeaths.
I'm here surrounded
by the vultures.
Picking out scraps,
from the carcasses
left to rot.
As the vultures eye me
menacingly.
Being thankful
for all that I've got.

Outside the walls,
beyond the gates,
in this place
where demons wait.
Knowing that soon
you'll meet your fate.
On the other side of Eden.
No snakes being deceiving.
Just empty plains,
harsh terrains,
and the pain
of this eternal grieving.
In that gated,
fenced off
beauty spot,
they have everything
that I've not,
but I've got
a rucksack,
a writing pad,
the shirt on my back,
and I'm happy with that.

No light

No light.
I walk into night,
into shadows.
I take my rightful place,
hidden in the fade.
I hide my face.
I stay in the darkness
where I can't be seen.
In the shade
of terror filled dreams.
No light.
Turn out the sun.
Walk into darkness
before my colours run.
I'm nothing,
a no one.
I say to nobody as my shadow
stretches away from me.

No light.
I fade as quickly
as a flame burns bright.
I need to stay
enshrouded by the night.
No one can see me, right?
And yet,
no light begets no life,
no right to walk head held high,
and I've worked
so damned hard to get here.
From a place so deep,
steeped in fear.
So, no I'll walk in the light
with my held high, I'll feel its brightness
the lightest kiss, the way it strokes my hair.

I used to rear up in fright
when I caught sight
of myself in the windows reflective light.
Now I see I'm just another person
going about their life.
Maybe not a model or anything,
but in my little world I'm happy,
and that's what I will always try to bring.

And deep in some long distant shadow.
I'll see my old self
looking back upon me,
through the reflective glare
of a window in streetlight flare,
and he will see someone
that has fought the demons of hell
and still walks free.
And he will think,
that is somebody I want to be.

Armed

I see through blood splattered eyes.
Is it any wonder that our flags
are seen with such deep despise?
When we cause so much strife
that even in our own four-walled houses
we are fed a sense of unease.
Distrust in anyone who sees
an alternative view,
or anyone who happens
to look slightly different to you.
Our forces armed to the teeth,
forcing their ways on other walks of life.
Making enemies is second nature,
when our leaders only look at ways to divide.
Arming genocide.

I see through blood tinted glasses.
Underclass masses,
seeing things with clear eyes,
but being drip fed lies.
Now let's make this clear. I love my country.
Not because of the people that want to divide,
plunder and rape other lands,
but to spite the blood running through their hands.
I love the diversity, the cultures,
the differences we all have.
All the stories this all breeds.
I just hate the way we bow to greed.
Feeding our desire for more
with everlasting wars.
Making enemies is second nature for sure.
Arming genocide shouldn't
be something we applaud.

I've been called
a bleeding heart,
had my voice silenced,
when all I want is to shout.
I've been told
that to make it in this world
you have to bow down.
Sell your soul.
Money is the only true goal.
Well, I say
fuck you very much,
but if I have to watch
ambulances get bombed,
hospitals destroyed,
children buried,
for your cause,
I say fuck this.
Stop the wars.
Arming genocide
is never worthy of applause.

I've been told,
don't cross the line.
Stop
before you
speak your mind.
Don't let
your emotions out.
Nah fuck it...
I'll shout. Ceasefire now.
If this is the good life,
I want to get off this ride,
or at least divert it to a better line,
one that doesn't involve
arming genocide.

Fragmental heart

Shards of red
adorn the floor.
Scattered, torn,
not beating anymore.
Nothing more
than ripped pieces
of a jigsaw,
where the edges
have been destroyed
and don't connect like before.

Surrounded by ashes,
burnt out reminders.
Desire and passions
stubbed out fires.
They once burned so bright
but then were doused
by the waters of insight.

These fragments
once lived
inside of me.
Now a gaping hole
for all to see.
A wound
stitched up hastily,
with papier-mâché
and strands
of memory.

The seagulls and me

Just me and the seagulls.
We have become equals.
Searching the bay in the morning sun.
Them for food.
Me, just for fun.
I watch on, breathing the salty air.
Not a care that I'm stood there
they squark and flap,
as they dive seeking scraps.

Low tide.
Morning sky.
Took a slow walk
down by the waterside.
Just me and the seagulls,
at ease,
wistful, peaceful. No noisy people.
Watching cascading churning water,
crash and fall.

Just me and the seagulls,
as morning calls.
Sun hugging the horizon.
Embracing it with golden light,
reflecting off the waves,
delightfully quiet.
Feeling the pull
of the water,
of the
sea.
Free
from all
that is troubling me.
Just me and the seagulls.

Blood on our hands

We have blood on our hands,
torn from the arteries of distant sands.
Taken from injected arms, sound the alarms,
sold in deadly arms, as this infected land burns.
I'm so pissed at the state of this.
Now I'm no anarchist
but this country wouldn't exist
without us, the populace.
So, don't try to make out that our thoughts
are just dead air or a foggy mist.
We stand for so much more than hate, blood and war.
We don't want your phoney division anymore,
stop with the hate it is beginning to grate
and I am way beyond thinking of the population
as the enemy in this debate.

Blood on your ledgers, filled out in red.
We fight the hedge funders, the bank lenders
the royalty sat on our legal tenders.
The governments that run us into debt
to cash in on our fears, spending the blood that we wept.
If we stand as one the house of cards crumbles at dawn.
Yet if we fall in line
we may as well be breathing our last,
ignoring the warning signs,
signing our death warrant in bloodlines,
another victory for the hateful elite class.
Stand, jump, scream if you want.
Throw a tantrum Mr Trump.
Mr Johnson do you have the nerve
to tell the population that you lied
or will you give that question a swerve?
Go on give it a try honesty is the best policy,
or you could always just run, find a fridge to hide inside.

Blood over our lands,
bathing the once green grass.
It's time to stop this attack at the pass.
Sunak quit pulling answers out of your ass,
when the sun begins to shine, it won't be from there.
The population will see through the clouds
of dirt that you encircle yourself with,
take back what is ours,
all you took, you stole. We didn't give,
it's not yours to control.

Fuck the government spin, there is no winning
in a war fought
over nothing
but greed and dishonesty.
For oil it's a travesty.
For profit it's a tragedy.
For the colour of skin or religious belief
it's worse than that it's an atrocity.
So, take your ill-gotten gains
your sinful funds and run,
fuck off and leave us alone.

There is blood running through the streets.
Flowing from the words that you preach.
The hateful bile that you spew.
So, pull up a pew.
We have some talking to do,
as we try in vain
to be as good as we can,
to see hope in our fellow man,
but it's so hard to do,
when we see pictures of you
and the hurt that you instigate,
through the words that you dictate.

90 Seconds till midnight

When are we
going to listen to sense?
Maybe now
is the time
to ask to repent?
Before long
it will be like
fixing the fence,
when the house
has already
blown away.
90 seconds,
the clock now sits.
That fan is slowly
getting coated in shit.
We are getting too close
to the final tick,
and I don't fancy
being vaporised.
I like my eyes
to not be filled
with blood red skies.

The warnings kept coming,
but we heeded not a thing.
Too obsessed were we,
with celebrity,
social media
and selfies.
Too focused on what we can get.
We let our planet fall into neglect.
Whilst our leaders hoarded weapons
of destructive force.
Enough to wipe us
from the very surface.

90 seconds till the bell chimes.
I quite liked passing the time
in the green hills of life,
but our selfish side,
our tribal warlike tide
kept crashing against those hills.
Always enough to make some blood spill,
never enough to heal those wounds.
And as the hands tick closer still,
it won't be fireworks exploding in the sky,
but the cries of nuclear fires,
the tears of fallout rain.
Simple question... *Why?*

The warning alarms sang in unison.
Unlike the people, no union.
Man against man,
and now we only unite to cry,
as we watch the fire rip apart the sky.
Whilst we plunder the oil fields,
sucking them dry.
Vampires of that black gold,
but that's a tale to be told
another time...

Oh, wait there is no other time,
the clock is starting to chime.

There is no more time.

FOUR

**I give my heart, still beating,
yearning, still burning
to store, forever with yours**

Poetic outlaw

He is
the poetic outlaw.
Plucking words
from rich
dictionary stores
and blending them,
into landscapes over which
you can pour,
to venture out into
and explore.
Taking the stars
from the sky,
and laying them down
into a verse
to shower your eyes.

He raids
vaults of letters,
a vast collection
of unearthed treasures.
Avoiding
the flying arrows,
to deliver a line.
Perhaps with
a rhyme.
A playful smile
on his lips,
as he bounds through
the world
of the rich.
Delivering
retribution
with a
well-timed
quip.

With his band
of merry men and women,
he always tries
to right the wrongs.
Tries to
find answers
to questions
that have
eluded him
for too long.
He scales
the castle walls,
like a squirrel
up a tree.
To explore, merrily,
the castle's
many mysteries.
The deepest dungeons.
A treasure trove
of golden words
to plunder.

He is the poetic outlaw,
with a hearty laugh
and a smile, he swings
from the high walls of the castle.
To deliver his refrains
with elegance and style.
As the sheriff
and his gatekeepers
try to explain
that this isn't poetry.
They want him locked in chains,
but his words are a skeleton key.
Freeing him from any lock.
They give him the freedom
to be who he wants to be.

A moment of stillness

In the noise and toil.
Recognise the beauty
in a moment
of silence.

Realise,
that
no words,
doesn't mean
no thoughts.

Sometimes
we get so caught
in the hustle,
that we ignore the beauty
of a delicate cuddle,
or a flower stretching out
to meet the sun.

And when
the world
is making tears run.

*Remember
that moment
of stillness.*

It doesn't mean
you are not hurting
from this man-made illness,
but that you are finding space.
To make peace your place
and to calm the storms
that whip around your headspace.

When the cries of hurt
are echoing
through every atom.
Remember
that stopping
for a moment,
won't stop
the good that
you've done.
It won't undo
the work
you put into
trying to make
the world
a better one.
Letting
it force you
to your knees
won't help anyone.

When it feels like
every word you shout
is just echoing back.
When nothing is stopping
the feedback,
the constant news
of attack after attack.
Stop.
Sit back for a second. *Breathe,*
and remember that taking a breath
won't make the messages
you send mean any less.
Self-preservation and self-love
doesn't mean you don't love others.
Taking a pause
just gives you the energy
to keep fighting for a cause.

Reverberations in the atoms

Are you aware?
Truly aware
of the atmosphere
that floats on the air?
The charged atoms.
Static, for a second,
before downpour comes
crashing from heaven.
The surge of sounds,
the drowning lands.
The booms that come
screaming loud.
The echoes are felt
far and wide.
From this storm
there is nowhere to hide.

Are you paying attention?
Really paying attention?
Listen to the rain
drops echo their reunion.
A call for rebellion.
End the pain.
They cry out in unison,
A shout of revolution.
As they join together
becoming one.
They flood
the streets,
to the sounds
of more
drumming home.

Are you listening?
Really listening?
To the way
the glistening
streets sing.
Their songs rousing
the very earth,
every worm
that ever turned,
now surges
towards the siren song.
The reverberations
felt in the atoms.
Small tremors
become explosions.

The wolf will roam

Hunger dripping
from the wolfs
snarled grin.
Ice in his belly,
stabbing,
painfully thin.
Scraggy fur,
Matted, worn bare,
but he won't give in.
He has a place out there.

Fire roaring
just out of view.
Hard to see the sparks,
slowly burning through.
Clouded eyes cover the flames,
but that fog will disintegrate,
dissipate into the wispy air.
When he finds his place
and lights his fire there.

The wolf, alone for now.
Alone for so long, but never bowed,
never cowered, he just doesn't fit in
with these particular crowds.
For they see not the joy inside,
nor his playful side. They see quiet,
so, they push him aside.
Not part of the pack,
he is not like us they bark,
he acts like a sheep.
Swims alone like a shark.

That lust for life,
is in every painful stride.
His pride sits
in knowing the journey
has been difficult, but that he
will never again hide.
It's in his loving nature,
his mournful howls.
The way he sings
to the moon on quiet nights,
just so she knows
she is not alone.
For wherever
her light lands
the wolf
will roam.

Paint the world

Sketchpad in hand,
you were always
painting the world,
but you never saw
the colour of the air.
The way the petals
waved, singing songs.
You only saw what
you knew was there.
Not the in-between
where the magic flows.

I only saw the blur
of a thousand worlds.
Never the clear outlines,
the fine lines, the details
so divine. I couldn't slow
my mind to take in the
breath of the wind.
So only ever saw
the stormy gusts
that flowed through
the images you'd see.

You never saw the look in my eyes.
The way they longed to be heard.
The way they wanted to be seen.
You only saw the details, the shapes,
never the shaded colours that blend.
You never saw the smile that
fell on my lips, when I saw you
slip into the room. Only the empty
canvas where the paint should drip.
You never saw the magic
brush away the gloom.

I never saw the way you
looked so closely. Trying
to find the me in the image
you see. I never realised
I'd hidden my feelings
so far away. Somewhere
not to be seen in the
light of day. Only to be
witnessed in dreams.

I never saw the way you
were asking me to stay.
I never learnt to read the lines.
My vision was always
blurred and undefined.

Crystalline

I want your crystalline shell
to melt around me.
I'll sup the waters until
they are no more.
To witness those eyes
looking to see,
to see you there
looking out to sea.
I'd see myself
in love with you,
and I'd see you falling
in love with me too.

I'd melt away your icy barrier,
the wall you use to protect.
Feel as its waters flow away.
So, you can see clearly, I'd project
an image onto your wall. Calling you to me.
I'd scrawl my name on the moon,
in magic ink that only you will see.

I want you to see
the world afresh
not like looking though
a smeared screen,
or a faded mesh.
I want you here with me.
In my arms.
Where I can keep
giving warmth.
To make every
last ice shard,
soften and thaw.

I'll burn as hot
as the sun for you.
I'd melt
right through
the walls
if it would help.
I'd combust
into a million fires
to keep you warm.
Even if it leaves me
just burnt-out ashes
on the floor.
If the last sight my eyes ever saw
was that smile beaming out,
I'd be happy to my core,
of that there is no doubt,
of this I am completely sure.

The embrace of an ocean

Water ripples over sand,
like fingers
teasing delicate skin.
Caressing
the hot sands beneath,
as the sun slides
into the dark reaches
of the water beside
these calming pebble beaches.
The moon takes its place,
to keep an eye
on the waters embrace.

The gentle flow
of the waves - to and fro,
like hearts in sync,
tuned to a frequency deep and low.
Somewhere in the waters below.
They breathe
across the shallows,
as inhibitions
start to sink.

Hot sand,
cooled
by the stroking hands.
Soft water over parched lands.
Waves kissing the beach,
with every motion.
The embrace of an ocean.
The loving waves.
Frothy mountains on salty seas,
delicately taking your heart away,
to swim in joy endlessly.

Headlight blinded

New worlds into which we grew.
New places to find,
streets and avenues.
Trees line the paths
like crowds watching a procession.
Taking respite in the shady night
in spite of the chill winds snappy bite.
Letting it dance in our minds
as it holds on tight.
Keeping us warm
as we explore the hidden world,
kept just out of sight.

This is no grand adventure,
no distant journey,
but the destination is worthy.
A joyride into the unknown,
an insight into how much
we've grown. Headlight blinded,
like distant eyes pierced by intense glows,
and the delights that the moonlight shows
on these streets, tree lined.

The road twists and turns.
It isn't a simple straight line,
it has dips and inclines.
There are parts where the traffic flows,
others where lights make it slow.
The view changes in just a few heartbeats.
City streets to green grass country seats.
If I could, I'd travel forever.
Drift from place to place,
with a heart by my side,
that would also embrace
the way the world changes
with every second, every breath we taste.

Pencil shavings

Pencil shavings.
That woody scent
stays with you.
From the days of your youth,
thinks the editor, as he scribbles
out whole portions of my life.
Crossing out
the bits that formed me.
All the interesting stories,
the late-night parties,
the loves that could have been…
True.
He rubs out the smiles, the laughter,
the happiness in certain views.
Leaves me with a page covered in solitude
and dusty eraser residue.

Written into a four walled room,
like the scratches that seem
hungry to consume
the walls. Just me and my thoughts,
which flow like angry waterfalls.

It's like whole portions
of my life have gone under
the surgeon's knife.
Cut from my past,
and into a bin have been cast.
Dead weight, dead end stories
with no beginning, middle or end.
But they all meant something to me.
At least, I think they did.
Is it too late to undo the damage they did?

The scent of pencil shavings.
Memories of school gates.
I was so far from cool,
was barely visible at all,
except when the bullies
needed a target of hate
to aim their barbed arrows at.
Unaware was I then, that
my mind was away elsewhere.
I followed the path. I did what I was asked.
What I was told.
But I never felt I belonged in this world,
like I was born into a place so cold.

As life's river trickles by
I find pages, torn reminders,
lives blown away like dust.
I couldn't trust. Myself, Anybody else.
I aimed to please, to make peace
with whatever beast was feasting
on my hopes and dreams.
This was just setting myself up to fall.
The one person
I wasn't pleasing was the one
that needed it most of all.
Myself.

Now I'm left with a tattered notebook,
my memories all twisted and mixed up.
My brain a jigsaw of pieces
that once fit before,
but now seem to only make sense
when I throw them out
in random shapes on the floor.

Beauty in fragmental skies

Beauty
in fragmented skies.
Something special
in the way
the sunlight catches the eye.
The way it pierces through
turbulent clouds,
never raising its voice
or making a sound.

Beauty
in wilting flowers.
Even if their colours are fading.
When the clouds open
and the heavens start raining
autumnal showers,
then once again
they will stand proud.
Though their life
may be draining.

Beauty
in the open air.
The way
a leaf floats
from the tree.
Sways majestically
as it dances
on the breeze.
It travels with ease.
Sun sparkles
from its
silken surface.
A memory
of a moment shared.

Beauty
in the ordinary,
in the
extraordinary.
The mundane
and the monumental.
The small and feeble.
The huge behemoths
and all in between.
There is beauty
everywhere in this world.
It's just hard to see
with eyes closed tight.
So, open them wide,
let them flood with light
and see all that is right.

Almighty pen

The crooked fingers of the hands of time
hold tightly, the almighty pen.
They sketch. Forever into parchment,
into atoms, all of time,
into every empty space.
Stretching arms out over the canvas.
Every new part, a new media,
squeezed, brushed, sprayed,
freehand, directed by the waves of life.
Pen, paint, pencil.
No need for a stencil.

A flourish as the whip-crack line is struck.
Charcoal fractures
against bone white background.
Soundlessly,
dust flows like black stars
against a snow sky, to the floor below.
Lines of black bestowed upon the page,
startlingly beautiful in contrast.
Creating new strands of life.
Sands of time sit dwindling
in the hourglass beside.

Drawing lines, time drawing on.
Directing the vast cosmic winds,
like an orchestra conductor.
With a flick of his wrist,
a new moon starts to shine. He sighs.
Sleeve billowing like leaves
on the trainline of time.
Stopping the work in its tracks.
He starts to perspire,
as his arm starts to tire.
The work is never complete,
a new sheet waits to be drawn.

Outside the dawn starts
to tear apart the darkness of night,
and the canvas is given
its first blast of sunlight.
In his tired aching state,
he smudges a bit.
Mangling the storyline,
a few lives at a time.
The eraser comes out
and rubs out countless lifelines.
Only oily feint marks left to remind.
Bloodline stains left on the page of time.
He scrawls a few hideous marks,
some blots on the canvas start to embark,
making a mess of his art.
Tearing apart his old heart.

Then he thinks of her.
The muse who visits
in those brief snatches of sleep.
In his dreams, the one who feeds his visions.
He pulls out some coloured crayons.
Taking his time,
with each line. Beauty,
to spellbind.
He takes many hours,
draws the curtains
then continues
painting flowers.

Human touch

The human touch.
Makes the galaxy twitch,
universes swirl, and into
a different world
we unfurl.
To curl up close,
and see souls,
in eyes
that don't close.

The scratch
of nails
tearing at skin.
The brush of
feather light
fingers down tensing spine.
Tingles the mind,
and heats the fires within.
As lips taste peace,
and teasing whispers invade
the minds creases.
Making sure
any pain ceases.

When two minds entwine,
so closely.
They feel as one whole, divine.
It's like feeling the storm
start to take hold.
Electricity
floods synapses,
pin prick eyes roll
towards the skies,
and heaven sings
a sea of sighs.

As passion bit lips press
against soft delicate flesh,
waves of happiness caress.
The human touch,
never to neglect.
Words flitter
through steamed air,
Hearts laid bare,
as we lay there.
Two souls breathlessly
breathing each other in deep,
only aware
of each other's stares,
and the sweet sweat-soaked
hours they shared.

Unrequited sighs

My thoughts will live
in the souls of lovers.
In their bones, their hearts
and their longing moans.
My tears will live in the
eyes of those
whose unrequited sighs
are heard only by ears
of the night.

My soul will walk you through
the graveyard of broken hearts.
Where dead love is littered like leaves,
and aching screams can be heard
grating against the breeze.
Where unrequited sighs go to die.
Their bodies kept out of sight,
a shroud worn as they are buried, lovelorn
under the dirt. A funeral of loves
that were never born.

Like the reaper
of unfulfilled love lives,
I walk a steady stride,
because I've been there
too many times to hide.
In that dead ground,
in that place,
where hurt sings so loud,
and I've tasted the tears falling
from my own eyes.
The tears cried
for love's unrequited sighs.

Enough to know

I know enough to know
that what I know means nothing.
That even if I'm a master at something,
there is still so much I could be learning.
I know that what makes me happy,
can sometimes make me sad too.
Something that feels good,
can be so very bad for you.

I know that if all
of my dreams came true,
I'd inevitably still end up feeling blue.
No matter how tall you feel
there is always room to grow.
I know enough to know
that when a storm blows through,
it won't stay forever.
It's just weather
and weather changes just like we do.

I don't know if tomorrow will be better.
I don't know if the rains will fall
heavier and heavier,
but I know
that I will survive a downpour
once in a while.
It will only get me wet,
I've been soaked a million times
and I haven't drowned yet.

A message to the stars

I send word to the stars.
Listen to our hearts.
I speak a word, just one word.
One that can mean so much.
It can light a fire,
make grown men blush
red with desire.
Cause fear to erupt,
in fear of it being missed.
It can make you feel
you have been kissed
by the lips of heaven.
It can turn your volume
up to eleven and continue turning.
I send that word, burning
right into the sky,
like a firework I let it fly.
Soaring and gliding through the clouds.
To let it shout so very loud.

I send a word.
Just a lone syllable.
It could end war, end hate,
make days and nights feel great.
It's almost biblical,
but this word isn't fictional.
It lives within us all.
In some it is more deeply hidden
but if we seek it out,
find that true joy,
is in giving.
Share it loud,
it will keep our world
spinning around.

I send a word
to the stars.
To orchestrate themselves
across the sky,
to pinprick the night
with hearts that shine.
I send the word to bring hope,
to regrow the beauty
in this world we share.
I send this word
to show I care.
I send a word
to overthrow
the damage
that men do.
To the stars above
I send one word
to you.

Love.

Love letters

Spill my love letters over the floor,
dispelling the lifeblood from my heart,
onto empty pages,
sent to deafened ears.
I want to write in flowers.
That way my bouquet of words
cannot be mistaken for flippancy.
I wish to spell words through
the scent of petals,
they will whisper
of the intense spell you hold over me.
So, you can smell it when you walk.
I want the rainbows to speak in sweet talk
let it flow out in colours so bold.

Let my love letters leak their diamond galaxies
to show us hearts and ruby stars.
In hope for ours to become full memoirs,
to be a universe, with no end.
I can think of no better way to spend
eternity, than staring into your eyes,
and seeing sun blessed cities.

Want to say,
in my own strange way,
that if my eyes were blinded
by a supernova burst,
that I'd be okay.
I'd remember
the miles traversed
as I have seen a sight
more beautiful
than anything
in this universe.

Let my love letters speak.
To show that, to me
you are more than rivers and seas.
More than mountain peaks.
More than skies through which we could fly.
Is it a trick of the light?
How can something shine so bright?
But I think I could give my life
to see that smile again tonight.

I want to spell my words
in touches from within,
soft brushstrokes on delicate skin.
Is it a sin to want to make you
feel like a queen, an angel in human form?
Is it wrong to want to hold you
on cold days and keep you warm?

Let my love letters
seek that place unique.
I want to explore the palace
that you hide within when your mind
is searching for answers.
The jewels that I'd find,
exploring the rooms inside.
I'd find treasures that shine,
stories written on parchment so fine.
Delicate to touch,
don't want to turn them to dust.
Crowned moments of glory.
The thoughts that swim in its pools and lakes,
the hope that walks across acres of garden landscapes.
Memories that haunt the estate,
fears left lonely, waiting at the gate.

The swiftest flick of a pen

Revolution begins
with
a single ripple.
A teardrop
in an ocean.
Cried because
the world has become toxic,
and the toxins
are making us hate
all that we
should be loving.

Slowly the
ripple spreads.
People feel that lingering dread,
the fingers pointing at your head,
in fearful gun symbolism.
They want you to stop thinking.
Execute any thoughts
before the injustice sinks in.

Revolution starts
with
a broken heart
tearing the sky apart
in despair at their loss.
No one seems
to count the cost,
and they notice not,
that the stars are fizzing out,
and the moon
is looking down on us
her face cross.

Our words could reach out,
but the ears
of the governing courts
are set on do not disturb. They will ignore.
Don't want to listen
to what we have to say any more.
So, instead, we have to shout.
They pray that we
fall victim to the games they play,
Manipulation, gaslighting,
outright lying.
Narcissistic abuses
of power.

Revolution begins
with the swiftest
flick of a pen.
A switched-on mic,
not the switchblade swing
of a knife,
nor an eye for an eye,
or a life for a life.
Revolution begins
when people
see the fakeness
of their smiles,
the hate
in their eyes
and see through their
wicked, vicious,
translucent lies.

Words rain

If words rained
on an empty room,
would there be
any sound at all?
Would it take on
the pitter patter
sound as it
makes land fall?
Would the echoes
reverberate
around the room?
Bouncing from
the very walls,
or would silence sit?
On his face
no emotion scrawled.

If words fell
in an empty forest,
would the
trees even care?
Would they be aware
of the liquid presence
of language
floating there?
Or would they
stare instead
at the great
star in the sky.
Just asking why?
As they beg for rain
to drizzle instead
of the words
that fizzle
trying to catch their eyes.

Words
without ears,
without eyes,
without audience sighs,
are just
faded memories.
Ghosts of time.
Stories told
to the empty sky.
They may make sense
of your mind,
but until aired
they are not
truly alive.

So, let my
words echo
through your bones.
Let them fracture
hearts of stone,
let them thaw
icy cores,
and let them
make tears leap
from eyes towards
wet floors.
Let them become
a part of you.
A part of us all,
and I'll sit and
listen to yours,
letting them become
a part of me too.
Learning to feel
our shared histories,
members of this
human family.

A sacred rhythm

She is a lullaby.
Her song sings me to sleep
through the darkest of nights.
Her words carry me through
this gravestone world of scares.
Her song turns my ice to blood
and my stony structure, to bone.
She weathers down my sandy exterior,
until fresh skin I wear.
In this moonlight home
she creates rivers, oceans,
and deep reflective seas.
She plants seeds in her words
that grow all through me.

A sacred rhythm
takes hold of my soul,
from this love I've been given.
She my lullaby with golden words,
like thin twine
to sew together the sections
of my patchwork mind.
Singing me to sleep,
slowing my heartbeat.
Until every drip of her words pour
like honey mixed with fine wine.

I'd let that sweet nectar
take me away.
I'd happily drift through
the soft satin light,
melting into the night,
from the ice cold of day.

She has a shimmering quality,
her words sing through me.
A fantasy, given life-like purity.
She cures me of any fear I hold.
Her skin I sink within
like a pillow embracing,
warming my heart
which has grown cold.
She sways
in and out
of view,
like a beam
of moonlight through clouds.
My lullaby. Never shouting loud.
A soft, lovelorn sigh
whispering to me.

On the darkest of nights.
When demons take the streets
and my vision is filled with frights,
she plants a forest of kisses
with every breath she breathes,
and I become one
of their floating,
falling leaves.
Forever living
on the melody.

A slice of home

I used to look upon
these streets with hurt.
All I could see
through these eyes,
were the tears I'd cried.
The bad times
glistened on
hateful pavements.

Smashed bottles lay
like
a permanent
reminder
of a life slowly
slipping away.
Where my blood spilled.
Scars still scratched
into the walls
where I fell,
and could
barely crawl.

Now I see the beauty
in every paving stone,
every arched alleyway.
The cobblestones lanes,
the market place.
The bustle of the clock tower where
we would spend forever
and a day,
standing around watching,
the slow crawling
hands of time
twisting idly away.

The old fountain
where we would
dance and play.
Skating on ice. The green fields
we would lay. Music swayed
through the airwaves.
Sounds from a long-forgotten
memory.

I see dreams of future,
flowing along the
pavement streams of yesterday.
The old and young standing together in harmony.
I hear songs being sung.
I see the joy of diversity in this city.
Taste the different traditions,
our cultures celebrated; our hearts elevated.
As new generations find all that tie us,
not find reason to feel misaligned,
maligned. I see graffiti showing life.
The train station where sad hearts pass time.
Waiting for love that doesn't arrive.
I see the green spaces, seemingly endless
seas of viridescent waves.

I no longer look upon
these streets with hate,
with hurt, or with fear.
I see where I belong.
Where the brickwork transports me
to a world, where the rain
sets forth storms of words.
I see the place that inspires pages to ignite.
I see a city of giving. The way we should be living,
and I look on with pride.

A whispered word to the rain

I spoke to the universe in vain.
Asking for it to light a flame,
I gave it a name,
and then asked
would it direct them
to my heart. I sent a signal,
in embers, to the stars.
A message written in sparks,
but it was never collected,
the sign was dismantled
before the message fully connected.
I whispered again to the rain.
Please let me share my soul.

I left my story
in a pile of books,
unread, unloved.
I let the work
stack up,
until it towered over me.
I wanted my words
to become solid, tangible.
Branches that would dangle over
and brush your hair.
I wanted you to know I was there
in the tangled threads of letters
that twisted
through the air.
That there is someone here
that sees you.
Not the image
you portray,
but the truth.

I spoke to the stars,
and they spoke back,
In silent glistening images,
of flowing futures.
They said, share your heart.
Worry not if it is misunderstood,
ignored or pulled apart.
The message sits within the universe,
the verse flits between
every pair of beating hearts.
A message to inspire love,
and light so many more fires
than just yours.

Centre stage

You take that stage,
poised to speak.
Tongue brushed
across dry unparted lips,
so, the words can slip.

Release.
Lightning crashes,
charged room, full of static.

Shimmery light fades blue.
Blinding burned retinas.
The air zips
swirling in and out of view.
Surging through every muscle.
The room has dulled it's hustle,
the lights have blown a fuse.
There is no one here,
just me and you. Alone.

You are speaking
directly to me.
Your words
so delicately
teasing their way free
from the lips
that imprisoned them.
Now they are out,
and drifting
into my ears.
Taking a route direct
to my heart.
To become a part,
making me whole again.

You let loose
more word gunfire,
more rapid
verbal flurries.
More perfectly
punctuated
playful pieces
of poetry.
They pour
into every opening,
then they sliver
and ooze,
through the
internal tunnel system,
until they come
to my brain stem region,
and they soothe.
Taking away
any discomfort or pain.

The mic so close
to your lips.
I wish to be there instead of it.
Letting the heat
of your words,
the beat of your heart,
course through my body.
A synced rhythm in time.
Your eyes look
directly into mine,
and I know you are
speaking to me alone.
There is no-one else here
in this weird
poetry twilight zone.

A storm and a sunny day

Like two sides of a flipped coin,
outgoing but introverted,
loud and quiet.
A storm and a sunny day.
A peace-loving riot.
Two sides of the same face,
one smiles. One hides
his lips away. Makes them thin,
barely visible to anyone.
I've become two parts
of one whole human.

I used to think that the poet
was the mask. That the anxiety
filled man was my natural fit.
The stage persona
was my escape
from feeling like an outcast.
But now I'm thinking,
maybe I had the tables flipped.
I'd misread the script
and all along. I was this.
I've realised recently
that the images have been
coming back showing negatives.
The reverse is true.
I'm more me, when
I'm speaking in truth.

The way the words fall,
like dominoes crashing
is really the way my thoughts,
like waves, are clashing.
I am that man.
The one that stands with a book in hand.
I am the one who would
try to outshine the sun if it meant
my words were the ones that would
make the world put down the gun.

I used to believe that I was nothing,
a nobody, a joke.
I lived up to these provocations
of my own brain.
I let them reign over me.
Instead of realising that
yeah, I'm a bit odd, quirky,
my mind works at a speed
that is sometimes a bit jerky.
But it works, and that's a start.
When I fire it up
it shines like a shooting star.

I used to be scared,
That people would not like me,
could not like me.
Well, they probably don't,
but I try to be
A good-hearted person.
So, if that makes me
someone to dislike,
then that's a relief I feel.
As I no longer have to deal
with you,
or anyone that follows
your views.

Our own private wonderland

Dreary haze
in the early morning
December rain.
Reawakened sun rays
dance across
tree branches,
bringing their apricity,
trying to break through
the gloomy greys.
To provide some brightness
to the day, before
leaving oh so quickly.

Bleak and frigid,
still and ridged.
The outside solid
like ice-packed
freezer stacks.
The air too cold to move.
To breathe.
It cracks as you
brush your hands
through
the thin glass sheen.
As you break
into a different reality.

A window into the snow globe view.
The forming of a new winter wonderland.
Ice rivers start to crystallise before you.
Water droplets freeze in time,
like the clocks have slowed to a stop
before your eyes, and the hands are too cold to drop.
As of now it's just glacial, inhospitable,
a window into a place that is inadmissible.

Characterless, colourless.
Nonetheless
it's a ponderous place to sit
and stare into the loneliness.
Seeing the thin strands
of beauty, the miniscule details
that pop with delicacy. The extraordinary
that mingles with the ordinary,
making order and the disorderly
become magically otherworldly.

The crisp reflections
from a cobweb.
Glistening shards hanging overhead.
Thin white dust on the glittery ground.
The way sound is muffled,
distant,
quiet, not loud.
I realise in that moment so profound,
that the winter wonderland
is almost complete, what a treat.
Just needs a few feet
of snow,
and you,
to make it
the perfect retreat.

The magic in raised lips

When she smiles,
sunlight fades away.
Dazzled and amazed,
it shades its eyes from the blazing light.
Electricity glows. Fuses blown.
Feint ghost light shimmers,
haunting the bulbs.
Lingering to catch a sight.
Candles flames wither away,
becoming vapour in the air.

When she smiles,
nothing else could compare.
Nothing else matters
in that single moment there.
Seeing the flowering
beauty blossom over her face.
Heart races. Never able to keep pace
with the way my thoughts taste.

When she smiles
It's not just in the lips,
her eyes raise to glance
as my heartbeat trips in a stumbled dance.
That gaze, could set a fire ablaze
in the coldest heart, in the darkest caves.
And when she smiles, I feel connected,
two halves of one. Two poles apart
but through the earth the poles are dissected,
like we are chained across time and space.
Wherever my heart lands,
her soul will embrace.

When she smiles.
She has questions
in her eyes,
she has answers
in her mind.
She sees the universe
and she sees
the love inside.
When she smiles
I know everything
is going to be
just fine.
Nothing can
hurt me
when this smile
beams down.

When she smiles,
no one could taunt away
the happiness,
nor haunt today,
trapping us.
I only see the
smile looming,
not any
creatures moving,
no demons lurking
or devil's working.

Under the moon
I'm free,
with this smile
watching over me.

Miss Aligned

I swear I saw you in a moon beam.
I'd know your face. I remember
you called to me one time in a dream.
Told me to close my eyes
whenever I needed to see.
For all I needed was already inside of me.
I close my eyes and I see you beckoning.
I see that look that makes me weak,
the one that makes my voice squeak,
when I am longingly trying to speak.

But I haven't met you yet.
Not in this space.
Time is flipped out of loop
but I know your face.
I've read the script.
This is the bit where we kiss.
But somehow
we don't even know we exist.
I know I know you,
I know you know me,
but it's in a different place.
An alternate reality.

But then I've seen glimpses,
in the edges, in the weird
fittings and fixtures.
There are fissures in reality.
Cracks in the universe.
I know you alright.
You just seem different
when I'm asleep at night.
You are the heart
I've felt beating in time,
and I'd hold yours tighter
than I'd ever held onto mine.

You are the wind, the air,
the warmth and the chill,
and when rest is needed
you are my sleeping pill.
You are the muse in the dark,
the pull on my heart,
the knock on my door.
The lock of hair on my floor.

I've seen you before,
both here and over there.
Though here you don't see me,
though you will one day, I'm sure.
Because time isn't a straight line
and sometimes
it needs to curve around
to get itself aligned.

Gatekeepers of the poetic word

This is not for academia
nor is it for awards or glory.
This is for the people,
our unique stories.
Poetry is for one and all,
you and me. Not to be hidden
behind a paywall at some university.

There are some that want us to cease.
Dusty white men, museum pieces
of an archaic world.
Gatekeepers of the poetic word.
They want our hearts to rot,
want our words to stop.
Replaced by wandering lonely clouds,
syllable counts, rhyme schemes.
The same tired sounds.
They want us to conform to the old ways.
not take an idea and play with new themes,
nor have fun with the art.
(I wonder what Shakespeare would say)

They see Instagram poetry as an affront,
spoken word, twisting of old ways,
somehow making the classics defunct.
Not reciting Shakespeare plays,
over and over again
relegates them in some way,
they will get lost in the mix
like we will all suddenly forget
that the classics exist.

But this is for our generation,
and the ones forthcoming.
Let's hear our words,
let the thoughts do the running.
Lest we forget,
in future times,
how life was lived
during these
interesting climes.

Let's not be pushed aside.
Our words are valid,
vital, important.
Beautiful, mesmerising,
haunting.
So, share them wide.
Let them ring out
true and loud.
Don't hide.
Be a poet
and be proud.

We don't talk

We don't talk.

We don't talk about
the hurt that
makes us want to shout.
We shut it inside.
We lock it down.

Stupid male pride.

We hide,
when it feels like the world
is grinding to a halt.
When you need to get out
but the door is bolted.
We can't share our faults,
or our desires,
the things that inspire us.

Stupid male pride.

Proud of what exactly?
The ability to sit in misery,
staring at the ceiling
watching clouds
of thought float nowhere.
Let our tears well up inside
until it finally gets too much.
We don't cry or show pain.
We bottle it up
and drink it back down again.

We don't talk.

We don't talk about our feelings
when smiles have all taken leave.
Grimacing at all the cards
life is dealing.

We don't share.

Like asking for help
makes us look weak,
and needing
someone to care,
makes us some
kind of freak.

We just push it down low.
Letting it fester.
Acting the clown, the jester.
Until it explodes,
our happiness corrodes.
Just sticking plasters
holding us together
and they are straining
from all the
acid blood that is raining.

Moonlight dream

Stretched across
moonshine sheets.
She speaks, softly.
In warming voice,
a northern tone greets
the southern cold.
It seems a tale told
in fiction of old.
A tale of love
that cannot be.
Parted by the stretch of time,
and the ancient weeping seas.

Stretched out
in the room of dreams
that bloom so delicately.
When the moon is full,
I see you,
and you are whispering
sweetly to me.
But the sounds
are drifting silently.
I want the southern downpour
to wash away
the northern uproar
that rocks me to the core.
I want that harsh weather
to batter my heart,
kick it back to life.
Give it a new start.

In my moonlit cocoon,
I look through the open window.
To see if you
are anywhere to be seen.
The scene that greets me
makes my smile beam.
A northern soul serenading
the serenity of a southern fool.
A moonlight dream swaying across
my tear clad eyes, like the tree of life.
It's limbs reaching out a magic kiss,
to give its love. To share in its bliss.

In moonlight grasp
I gasp at the clasp
you hold around my heart.
The light you impart.
I want that northern sweetness
to fill me with goodness.
Take the southern chill
from my skies and instil
some heat into my heart.
Set a fire for me
and we can lay together
beside the flames that rise.
Watch the embers embark,
dancing before our eyes.

Lantern holder

That smile could make
a whole room sing.
So beautifully
alluring.
It pulls you in.
It beams like the sun
shining all over everyone.
It makes the day
feel like a second spinning away,
as you wish for the hands of the clock
to stop and let time just witness
the wonders for a momentary gaze.
Time would stand
hands outstretched
as if in praise.

Eyes that speak so many languages,
each one enticing,
like a cake with popping candy icing.
Making you gasp
at the magic she is supplying.
They make you fall to your knees,
a beggar or a pilgrim
praying for her sanctuary.
With a flutter she makes
your heart and voice stutter.
All you can provide
is a barely audible mutter.
But her glance brings peace,
starts to make you feel at ease.
In her company you feel release.

But in her words and thoughts,
is where her true beauty unfolds,
soothing wounds with her heart and soul.
A doctor, or nurse,
a blessing,
never a curse.
But much more.
When the path is lost
and the skies go dark,
she is a lantern holder
pointing the way to embark.
She listens
when no one else will.
A therapist,
not just there with a pill,
but with a hand to hold
when the world is feeling unreal.

Her light so blinding,
on those dark cold nights.
Keeps you safe
when a fall would end your life.
That smile,
happiness that glows,
like a star
in the darkest night.
A beacon so bright.
She never hides it away
always letting her light
shine through.
To remind you of day.

Why did the poet cross the road?

Why did the poet cross the road?
The question asked.
No answer told, not written in bold.
Just a lengthy look inside the mind,
as it slowly unfolds. Unwinding,
trying to get two pieces to tie,
to make a little sense of
where the road came from
and why.

Why did the poet cross the road?
To ascertain for certain
that the road really exists
and isn't just a metaphor
for the way life twists?
To see if they can persuade it to
become a river instead,
waterways always
open up thought streams
in the poet's head.

Why did the poet entertain
that the road needed crossing?
Was it a way to share a tale of pain?
Or to show love in a different,
more flowery frame?
Was it to show the end is
but the beginning, as it
cycles around again?
Or was it to reach a place
where he could look back upon
where his journey had begun,
from a different perspective?
Like looking down upon it
from space.

The whites of your eyes

Snow kissed memories
under those jewels of the sky.
I see the whites of your eyes
and the deep dark irises
with worlds held inside.
You invite me in. *With a blink.*
I open the door just a chink
and step over the threshold
to the space within.

I set foot in a world of beauty.
Where scintillating diamond moons
shine down upon me.
This land we walk on,
this land of rich red ruby,
emerald skies and the rivers
of silver shining skyward.
The starlight reflecting back,
like snowdrops in a dream.

If heaven could ever match the scenery,
then maybe I'd believe. I'd let that
choral music wash me in its shimmery waters
and swim with its most beautiful daughter.

A world reflecting
every sizzling atom
of your lustrous being.
Raspberry ripple thoughts
swirl through the strawberry hills
and tangerine valleys of this land.
So pleasant a place to roam.
A wonderland I wish to call home.

The feeling of a kiss

I like the sound
love makes when it walks into a room.
A song singing summer fields to life.
To see the butterfly hearts and the smiling flowers
swaying and dancing in tune.
I love the feeling of a kiss,
as it releases trapped lips
with sweet tasting electricity, zipping
like a storm that is only there to please.
Teasing lips gently apart,
to breathe the finest fresh breeze.
The cleanest air your mind could ever conceive.
And during those brief times
when things go astray,
the beauty of shared whispered apologies,
swirling circling away, the whirling hurt
chased like children at play.

I love the feeling of
whispered sweet nothings.
As they brush your cheeks,
feather soft, they speak
to every single dimple and pore.
They caress every stowaway
slowing heartbeat
that you have stored up. Ready to erupt.
That burst of joy.
As your heart starts to race again.
Embracing every moment.
Knowing that it's real,
that showing your soul
and the deeper parts within
are not going to leave you alone in
this field of love.

I love the way words
don't always need to be used.
Sometimes telepathy is real.
How two hearts
can just know
when the other is yearning.
Like when you pick up
your phone
before it rings
and then she starts calling.
The magic at work
as the earth is turning.
It can be hard to navigate.
Sometimes you have to
find the right keys
to unlock the doors of fate.
Or just sit and wait.
Your time isn't ready.
It's in the oven baking.

Peace, love & poetry

Peace, love and poetry.
These words I place
so delicately
at the foot
of every
poem,
like seeds.
Ready to sprout roots
and start the next poem growing.

Peace, in oneself
and without.
We need to seed the world
with hope, not with doubt.
We should cease the endless greed.
The division it breeds.
We struggle to keep our feet on the ground
letting the hateful waters flood around,
until we are underneath
struggling to breathe.

Love, it's a cliche
but it is all we need.
Love is all around, we should feed.
Let it seep inside, wash away the hate,
creeping, oozing through tarnished blood.
Let it clean the stains,
that are thick and stuck tightly to our veins.
Let love win, it's our only chance.
Stop fearing difference,
in our skins we are all one.
Share that love with everyone,
don't see it as us and them,
haves and have-nots,
all that matters is within.

Poetry, helps these thoughts air,
and once they
are out there,
floating in the atmosphere,
they may rain down,
wash away
some of the fear.

The rains may be
painful at times,
that's just the goodness
washing away
the itchy years of grime.
They may tickle you,
cause you to cry
tears of laughter.
They may sting as they
uncover pain, kept long hidden,
but these emotional waters
will heal us.
So, we can finally
learn to be free.

When apocalypse comes

When the apocalypse
looms high.
Fire in the sky,
towering over us.
I won't come out swinging,
my arms will be held by my side.
I won't shout in anger
tearing down any buildings in my stride.

I'll be singing songs
that speak of freedom.
Unshackling restraints,
I'll be helping to release,
those chained in misery.
I'll be handing out
flowers of peace,
not ways to increase
the pain and suffering.
I'll be talking about the beauty
of rivers and seas.

When the apocalypse is nigh,
I won't sigh,
or try to gain from others
mournful cries,
I'll be there,
arms held by my side.
No weapons,
just a heart full of verses,
with words
that speak of love across
vast universes.

I'll keep singing of peace,
not swing a fist,
nor aiming to bring pain.
I'll sing for the seas,
the beauty they give me.
I'll sing to the moon,
the stars, the sun.
I'll sing for you.

And to those
that keep us cowering,
up high in their ivory towers.
I'll sing of redemption.
As they will be first
to feel the flames,
of their own temptation.
When the skies
come crashing
in fiery rain.

Silencing of the hum

The hum, it seemed,
had ceased.
Does that mean
that so too
had the
unshaply beasts?
Was it now
safe to walk
these midnight streets?
Knowing that you
were not going
to end up
on a dinner plate,
in a hall
full of monsters
at some
stately feast.

But the hum had been
replaced
by silence.
Not just quiet,
not just a lack of noise.
But a void. *No sound at all.*
A vacuum, like space.
If you screamed no one
would hear you call.
As soon as you breathe
the sound stops dead on your lips.
Step forward,
not a grain of gravel
splits the silence,
not a single rip
in the heavy fabric of saturninity.
Just emptiness falling into infinity.

The hum.
Nothing but a forgotten sound.
Warned when danger was around.
Now the silence has come.
There is nothing.
Nothing that can be done.
You can feel the lingering dread.
You feel the talon-like fingers
tearing your soul to shreds,
you know its ripping
the flesh from your head,
but the sound is buried deep inside.
You can't even scream.
The sound arrives
at your lips, then just bleeds
into emptiness.
Not a single slip, not a drip.
Not a flicker of life in a candle wick.

The hum had gone, left us,
and taken the background noise with it.
Now just empty silence sits.
Heavy. Aching,
mind penetrating silence.
Climbing inside
and rewiring your thoughts.
Until all you feel
is uncomfortable in your skin.
Then it starts to itch.
Making you scratch.
Shedding layers
to feed its invisible grin.

That was when
the menacing
laughter began...

Thank you for reading.
If you have enjoyed this book
then please leave a review
where purchased.
Peace, Love, and Poetry.
Kyle.

The Night Watchman
(2019)
ISBN 978-1797484419

"When day ends, and night falls
When the sun leaves the sky, and darkness calls
The watchman sits, his duty to observe
Protect the dreams, of those who deserve"

This poetry collection takes us on a journey into the murky depths of the night. Down dark alleyways, through disused wastelands.
The beasts are out in force, who will hear our calls?
it will be a long night, but the watchman is looking out for us all.

"The Night Watchman is a thought-provoking carousel of dreams, rage and sympathy all at once. Rebellious but kind-hearted, powerful and fresh. A relevant collection to current problems.
It is an observant and raw book of poems that I would recommend for anybody with a full five stars. If you need proof that poetry is just as vital, if not more vital to literature today than it's ever been, here is proof."
Realistic Poetry International

Seasons
(2019)
ISBN 978-1689340434

"Seasons keep turning, like the hands on a clock
tick tock, the pendulum rocks, as we take stock
days pass, the weather changes on the fly
spring into summer, a gull cries into autumnal skies"

This thought-provoking poetry collection touches subjects ranging from love and loss to addiction and mental health issues.
Taking a tour through the seasons.

"Author Kyle Coare is an exquisite Poet and Word Artist that truly knows how to bring words and the world to life through poetry, and this collection of animated poems is more than proof!
Reader's will experience the rush of each season while traveling through its pages, from summer to winter, to spring to fall, in which we realize just how well life and people mirror the concept and cycle of the seasons and how they change. This book is one of our favourites from the Author. Kyle Coare is both an artist and a poet in this collection, creating specially for the heart, mind, body, and soul. Beautiful work."
Realistic Poetry International

Lone Wolf
(2020)
ISBN 979-8613023912

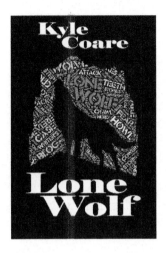

"Wolves howl, they don't cower from the storm
they prowl, they don't crawl or fear the swarm
the lone wolf takes a step from the pack
But don't stand too near, he's ready to attack
Snarling, his teeth glint in the moonlight
The pale spark of hope in the night"

Join the wolf on his path, as he tries to make sense of the world, we inhabit. Seeking answers in the aftermath of a wrecked planet. Through the urban wilderness of love and hurt, anxiety and mental illness. Against the backdrop of an apocalyptic nightmare world, on the brink of collapse.

"It is very apparent that many heartfelt efforts went into this book; the author bares their heart on their sleeve. Thus, we do believe that many reader's hearts will be equally captivated – just as much as ours were. the style of writing which is seen within Lone Wolf seems quite unique and refreshing. Collections like these are a rare breed, and we recommend adding this one to your shelves as soon as possible"
Realistic Poetry International

Headfirst into the storm
(2021)
ISBN 979-8526622288

"The rain poured like we had angered the gods
thunder roared lightning struck the brick and stone facades
of the halls that we sat, enclosed inside
nowhere else to hide
we heard the drumming downpour
and we bunkered down fortified"

Feel the cold chill of fear, the icy sting of pain as we run
headfirst into the rain, through a year that never was,
2020 its given name.
Embark on an emotional joyride, let the weather guide
ducking and diving for cover as the driving rains fall
we search for calm trying to find the sunshine after the storm.

"This poetry is rooted solidly to the ground, emotionally reaching down
to hell, but at the same time with moments that can lift the soul.
it could easily be a modern-day Decameron. With 105 poems about life,
mental illness, virus, lockdown, lost love, failed relationships and more
than the odd political and social commentary that lays it on the line.
This is no nonsense, powerful poetry, written to be spoken, not shouted
from a podium, maybe at speaker's corner to get attention or from be-
hind a news desk, because folks what's here is real, it's happening and
we have a responsibility to listen, understand and act."
Carl Butler (Dark Poetry Society)

In Shadows
(2022)
ISBN:979-8448585333

"Something is coming,
its hiding in the dark.
In shadows, it is stalking,
ready to stop your heart"

This poetry collection will take you deep into the bowels
of hell, Through its lava filled mouth, where demons howl.
217 pages of horror themed poetry storytelling.
Filled with humour, scares, light and shade.

"Kyle has once again left us spellbound and on the edge of our seats
with this tantalizing collection. The various forms of proses and poetry
take us through the innermost workings of the unexpected ride that is
life. Your mind and soul will dance in grace and reverie, as you move
through its pages. This incredible title is immersive, in every aspect.

"In Shadows" is an exquisitely crafted masterpiece — a micro adventure
that is a delight to experience; don't delay! If you're looking for material
built with genuine care that can offer soft introspection and the thrill of
discovery, this latest treasure from Kyle is the book for you!"
Realistic Poetry International

Torn Pages: Scraps of midnight
(2023)
ISBN: 979-8375840512

"I bleed internally
from invisible scars.
I want to scream so loudly
I shatter the stars"

Torn Pages is a collection of poems, ripped from the heart, torn from the soul and cut from the mind of poet/author Kyle Coare. Each of the 100+ poems takes you deep into different aspects of life, from love and pain to health and hope. Also touching on struggles with mental health, loss and with society as a whole, whilst always trying to remain playful.

"Any poet this consistent with their skills is destined for greatness!"
Experience the soulful power and journey into the depths of life's emo-
tion through heartfelt words. Feel pain, love, hope and even learn to ac-
cept yourself with this honest & raw collection of poems. Let these pages
become your silent companion as you discover healing and acceptance
with every line.
Torn Pages is absolutely a beautiful piece of work. It's a dreamy, en-
chanting exploration into a broken world. The poems draw you in and
you feel like you are a part of the journey. Torn Pages is definitely worth
every penny, it will stay with us for a long time. We've been reading this
amazing book all day and we can't seem to put it down!!"
Realistic Poetry International

Endless Nightmares
(2023)
ISBN: 979-8394691119

*"The shadows warned us,
but we didn't heed their cries"*

Kyle Coare brings you more dark tales, more twisted nightmares, in this spiritual successor to In Shadows. Scary visions mired in the shadows. Lurking beasts and crooked wonders. Shady lanes and darkened corners. Apparitions rising from the grave. The shadows warned us, but we didn't hear their cries. The shadows warned us, at the cold dark end of day. The shadows warned us and now the beast is on his way...

*"Endless Nightmares is an exceptional, must-read book of poetry
that will give readers nightmares with its vivid and haunting horror-
themed imagery,
a true testament to the author's unparalleled talent, dedication, and skill.
Overall, the book is a heart stopping and addictive experience,
leaving readers excited for what Kyle Coare will create next."*
Realistic Poetry International

Carpe Noctem
(2023)
ISBN: 979-8394691119

"Carpe Noctem – Seize the night, reclaim the dark as friend"

Into the beauty of dreams, the moonbeams laying fairytale lights over the alleyways and streets. Night has its terrors, but it has love also, so follow as Kyle guides the reader on a journey through the night.

"Kyle Coare has a remarkable talent for tugging at your heartstrings,
and in "Carpe Noctem," he explores themes that are lighter
in comparison to some of his earlier works. This time around,
the poems are brimming with love and hope, delivering an emotional
impact that leaves you yearning for more. It's clear that Kyle possesses
a raw skill and a deep love for poetry, evident in the vivid imagery and
metaphors woven throughout the book.
"Carpe Noctem" stands out as one of his most outstanding works to date
His voice is strong, his words powerful and precise,
making "Carpe Noctem" a must-read for poetry enthusiasts."
Realistic Poetry International

ABOUT THE AUTHOR

Kyle coare is a poet and author from Leicester, England.
His work veers between enchanting beauty and dark nightmares. Bringing
new worlds to life, be they horror landscapes, or dreamy hideaways.
He likes to combine storytelling and poetry, often pointing a spotlight on the
world we inhabit. With some humour and some dark edges but is just as
comfortable writing about love and hope, as he is loss and hurt. His work
can be dark, but through the darkness there is always light.
He has performed at various spoken word events and slams and was the
2022 2funky/Some-Antics slam winner.
He also co-hosts the monthly poetry night Get Mouthy in Leicester.
His work has also featured numerous times on BBC Radio, and Pukaar
magazine.

www.facebook.com/wordsandfluff
Https://linktr.ee/wordsandfluff

Printed in Great Britain
by Amazon

38524792R00178